Interdisciplinary Feminist Perspectives on Crimes of Clerical Child Sexual Abuse

In recent years the sexual abuse of children in religious institutions has gripped the Western world, as churches, governments and civil society attempt to come to terms with the magnitude of widespread historical abuses. Questions continue to be asked about why it is that perpetrators were able to offend repeatedly and with impunity; what is it about institutions that facilitate or foster abuse; and why have survivors of abuse often been treated inadequately by diverse national and international justice and political systems throughout the last century? This volume makes a significant contribution to international understandings of the vexed and sensitive 'wicked problem' of child sexual abuse in religious institutions. The chapters in this volume are written from a range of feminist disciplinary responses, including law, criminology, anthropology and history. Together, they provide important historical context for the current social and political interest in clerical sex crimes. They examine political and legal avenues for redress for survivors of these crimes and critically examine the ways in which church cultures position clergy and clergy offenders in relation to victims.

The chapters in this book were originally published in a special issue of the *Australian Feminist Law Journal*.

Kate Gleeson is Senior Lecturer in Law at Macquarie Law School, Australia. She has published extensively on the regulation of bodies, sexuality and reproductive practices. She has particular expertise in justice for crimes of institutional and historical child sexual abuse in Australia and internationally.

Timothy Willem Jones is Senior Lecturer in History at La Trobe University, Melbourne, Australia. He is a cultural historian of sex, gender and religion in modern Britain, Australia and the USA.

Interdisciplinary Feminist Perspectives on Crimes of Clerical Child Sexual Abuse

Edited by
Kate Gleeson and Timothy Willem Jones

Routledge
Taylor & Francis Group
LONDON AND NEW YORK

First published 2019
by Routledge
2 Park Square, Milton Park, Abingdon, Oxon, OX14 4RN, UK

and by Routledge
52 Vanderbilt Avenue, New York, NY 10017, USA

First issued in paperback 2020

Routledge is an imprint of the Taylor & Francis Group, an informa business

British Library Cataloguing-in-Publication Data
A catalogue record for this book is available from the British Library

ISBN 13: 978-0-367-58520-4 (pbk)
ISBN 13: 978-1-138-32451-0 (hbk)

Typeset in Times New Roman
by codeMantra

Publisher's Note
The publisher accepts responsibility for any inconsistencies that may have arisen during the conversion of this book from journal articles to book chapters, namely the possible inclusion of journal terminology.

Contents

Citation Information

The chapters in this book were originally published in the *Australian Feminist Law Journal*, volume 41, issue 2 (December 2015). When citing this material, please use the original page numbering for each article, as follows:

Introduction
Feminist Contributions to Justice for Survivors of Clerical Child Sexual Abuse
Kate Gleeson and Timothy Willem Jones
Australian Feminist Law Journal, volume 41, issue 2 (December 2015) pp. 201–205

Chapter 1
'Perhaps Some Writing: And a Record of my Age'
Lewis McCabe
Australian Feminist Law Journal, volume 41, issue 2 (December 2015) pp. 207–211

Chapter 2
The Royal Commission into Institutional Responses to Child Sexual Abuse: Learning from the Past
Fiona Davis
Australian Feminist Law Journal, volume 41, issue 2 (December 2015) pp. 213–218

Chapter 3
Graceful Remedies: Understanding Grace in the Catholic Church's Treatment of Clerical Child Sexual Abuse
Kate Gleeson and Aleardo Zanghellini
Australian Feminist Law Journal, volume 41, issue 2 (December 2015) pp. 219–235

Chapter 4
Sin, Silence and States of Denial: Canon Law and the 'Discovery' of Child Sexual Abuse
Timothy Willem Jones
Australian Feminist Law Journal, volume 41, issue 2 (December 2015) pp. 237–252

Chapter 5
Reparation for Betrayal of Trust in Child Sexual Abuse Cases: The Christian Duty of Care, Vicarious Liability and the Church of England
Kim Stevenson, Judith Rowbotham and Jason Lowther
Australian Feminist Law Journal, volume 41, issue 2 (December 2015) pp. 253–270

Chapter 6

An Unexpected Path: Bankruptcy, Justice and Intersecting Identities in the Catholic Sexual Abuse Scandals
Meredith Edelman
Australian Feminist Law Journal, volume 41, issue 2 (December 2015) pp. 271–287

Chapter 7

Giving Voice to Narratives of Institutional Sex Abuse
Shurlee Swain
Australian Feminist Law Journal, volume 41, issue 2 (December 2015) pp. 289–304

Notes on Contributors

Fiona Davis is Postdoctoral Research Fellow in the National School of Arts at the Australian Catholic University (ACU). Her current research explores social welfare enquiries in Australian history.

Meredith Edelman is PhD Scholar at the Regulatory Institutions Network at the Australian National University, Canberra, Australia and is supervised by Professor John Braithwaite. She holds a Juris Doctor from the University of Southern California, Los Angeles, USA and a Bachelor of Arts from Earlham College, Richmond, USA.

Kate Gleeson is Senior Lecturer in Law at Macquarie Law School, Australia. She has published extensively on the regulation of bodies, sexuality and reproductive practices. She has particular expertise in justice for crimes of institutional and historical child sexual abuse in Australia and internationally.

Timothy Willem Jones is Senior Lecturer in History at La Trobe University, Melbourne, Australia. He is a cultural historian of sex, gender and religion in modern Britain, Australia and the USA.

Jason Lowther is Associate Professor and Senior Lecturer in Law at the University of Plymouth, UK. His research interests include environmental law, underwater cultural heritage law and policy, tort law, legal pedagogy and drugs and the law.

Lewis McCabe is a survivor of institutional child sexual abuse and in 2012 made a submission to the Victorian Parliamentary 'Inquiry into the Handling of Child Abuse by Religious and Other Non-Governmental Institutions'.

Judith Rowbotham is Visiting Research Fellow at the University of Plymouth, UK. Her role is to work with, and, where required, to advise and mentor, staff at the University of Plymouth, drawing on her established expertise across the fields of history, law and criminology in particular.

Kim Stevenson is Professor of Socio-Legal History at the University of Plymouth, UK. Her research interests include historical and contemporary aspects of the criminal law with particular emphasis on sexual offences, sexuality, morality and violence.

Shurlee Swain is Professor of Humanities at ACU. Her work has informed several of the recent Australian enquiries into institutional abuse. She is the team leader of the Historicising Social Policy Program within ACU's Historical Research Concentration.

Aleardo Zanghellini is Professor of Law and Social Theory at the University of Reading, UK. His areas of interest are legal, political and moral philosophy; law, gender and sexuality; and socio-legal and cultural studies.

Introduction: Feminist Contributions to Justice for Survivors of Clerical Child Sexual Abuse

Kate Gleeson and Timothy Willem Jones

The scandal of systemic institutionalised child abuse by clergy and other church personnel continues to unfold across the globe with unremitting effect. Northern Ireland is the latest among a number of countries to establish a National Inquiry into Historical Institutional Abuse, in 2014. That Inquiry has found that the region's most notorious 'paedophile priest', Father Brendan Smyth, was 'known to' police and treated by psychiatrists from the 1970s, before finally being convicted in 1994 of over 100 assaults on children in the Republic of Ireland and Northern Ireland over 40 years.[1] As nation after nation grapples with the magnitude of historical abuse in institutions including churches, questions continue to be asked about why it is that perpetrators were able to offend repeatedly and with impunity; what is it about institutions that facilitates or fosters abuse; and perhaps most chillingly: why have survivors of abuse often been treated inadequately and with disdain by diverse national and international justice and political systems throughout the last century?

The sexual exploitation of children has been a concern of feminists at least since the time of the suffragettes, but the political acknowledgement of abuse endemic in institutions is a defining theme of the twenty-first century. The belated and piecemeal justice beginning to be delivered to survivors through national commissions and other public inquiries has been made possible only by the relentless work of feminists, activist and academic, in framing the issue as one of public, not private, concern. As Shurlee Swain documents in this volume, 'child sexual abuse' was (re)discovered in the West in the 1970s, a discovery made possible by feminist critiques of patriarchy and gender, domestic violence and sexual assault.[2] Named and diagnosed by doctors in 1969 as a condition to be treated medically and individually,[3] child sexual abuse

---

[1] BBC News 'Historical Abuse Inquiry: Fr Brendan Smyth "Could Have Abused Hundreds of Children"' 22 June 2015 <http://www.bbc.com/news/uk-northern-ireland-33223162> Accessed 26 August 2015.

[2] This argument was made first in: Olafson Erna, Corwin David and Summit Roland 'Modern History of Child Sexual Abuse Awareness: Cycles of Discovery and Suppression' (1993) 17(1) *Child Abuse and Neglect* 8.

[3] De Francis Vincent *Protecting the Child Victim of Sex Crimes Committed by Adults* American Humane Association Denver 1969.

was exposed most dramatically as a social function of gendered power relations by Florence Rush's groundbreaking presentation on 'The Sexual Abuse of Children: A Feminist Point of View' at the 1971 New York Radical Feminists Rape Conference.[4] Focused first on abuse within the family and combating Freudian theories of seduction and fantasy, feminist framings of child sexual abuse were developed and expanded, revised and made more nuanced in a process enabled simultaneously by the novel sexual frankness and new legal discourses of children's and victims' rights from the 1970s to now. By the 1980s, child sexual abuse had been made an issue of mainstream international legal and political concern, and was named as a crime in the 1989 United Nations *Convention on the Rights of the Child*.[5] By this time, the spectre of abuse in institutions and religious organisations had begun to make itself known. All the while, throughout this period, feminists have had to contend with reactionary discourses, regimes and movements organised to deny the prevalence, nature and effects of abuse.

It was in the 1990s that the figure of the 'paedophile priest' assumed the stature of a 'folk devil' internationally — a distinct, pathological psychic entity.[6] But it is now evident that, as Timothy Willem Jones's article[7] in this volume details, numerous churches were internally addressing sex offenders well before the mid-1980s, when high-profile criminal and civil court cases in the US brought the Catholic Church in particular to the point of public crisis. The internal responses of churches have since been revealed to have been inadequate and often inappropriate in their focus on remedying scandal to the profound detriment of enabling justice and preventing crime.[8] If not for the relentless work of survivors and their advocates, the inadequacies of such responses may never have been exposed and begun to be addressed by governments and the law.

The significance of feminist interventions in this history is illustrated by juxtaposing the early responses of the Australian Catholic Bishops' Conference (ACBC) and the feminist organisation, CASA (Centre Against Sexual Assault) House. In 1988, the ACBC established a working group to formulate the Church's Protocol for Dealing with Allegations of Criminal Behaviour [sexual offences], in response to similar initiatives by bishops in the US. At around the same time, CASA House began its own investigation into sexual violence in Australian churches. In collaboration with the Women, Church and Sexual Violence Project Advisory Group of the Victorian Council of Churches it issued a *Pastoral Report to the Churches on Sexual Violence against Women and Children of the Church Community*, published in 1990. While the ACBC deliberations were conducted in secret, and the confidential 1988 Protocol has since been criticised for being overly concerned with institutional liability and insurance risk, the published CASA report confronted churches, governments and the general public with the experiences of women and children who were the victims of

[4] Rush Florence *The Best Kept Secret: Sexual Abuse of Children* McGraw Hill New York 1980.
[5] United Nations General Assembly *Convention on the Rights of the Child* 20 November 1989 United Nations Treaty Series Vol. 1577 p.3 (UNCRC).
[6] Jenkins Philip *Pedophiles and Priests: Anatomy of a Contemporary Crisis* Oxford University Press Oxford 1996.
[7] Jones Timothy Willem 'Sin, Silence and States of Denial: Canon Law and the "Discovery" of Child Sexual Abuse' (2015) 41(2) *Australian Feminist Law Journal* 237.
[8] Parkinson Patrick 'Child Sexual Abuse and the Church: A Story of Moral Failure?' (2014) 26(1) *Current Issues in Criminal Justice* 119.

sexual violence in churches. It was a groundbreaking document in the articulation of child sexual abuse in religious institutions. CASA's 'breaking the silence' would ultimately contribute to the response of the Victorian government of Australia establishing a number of inquiries into child abuse including the crucial 2012 Victorian Parliamentary Inquiry into the Handling of Child Abuse by Religious and Other Organisations [the Victorian Inquiry] examined by a number of authors in this volume.

There are now fourteen CASAs funded by the Victorian state government. They provide services to women, men and children who have experienced sexual assault in various contexts. CASAs work to ensure that victim/survivors have access to comprehensive and timely support and intervention to address their needs. Many CASA clients have been sexually assaulted by members of religious and secular institutions. The cover of this special issue features a photograph of Carolyn Worth, a CASA manager who has worked for over two decades as an advocate for victims/survivors. She explains that:

> over the past twenty years CASA has tried hard to engage with various religious organisations when it has been clear that there is a problem with predators. This has been a difficult activity and not particularly successful until the last few years.[9]

Worth also notes that the Victorian Inquiry 'changed the whole climate in Victoria in relation to people's responses to institutional abuse and made it easier to engage with organisations'.[10] She looks forward to an open, systematic approach to sexual abuse in the future.

This special issue of the *Australian Feminist Law Journal* grew out of a workshop funded by the Academy of Social Sciences in Australia held at La Trobe University in September 2013. The workshop was convened on the theme of 'Religion and Sexual Politics in Postsecular Australia', involving scholars from a range of disciplines in law, the humanities and social sciences considering the relationship between sex and religion in secular society. It was then almost a year since the then Australian Prime Minister Julia Gillard had announced the establishment of a national Royal Commission into Institutional Responses to Child Sexual Abuse (the Royal Commission), analysed by Fiona Davis in this volume. A number of papers at the 2013 workshop, directly and indirectly, addressed religion, childhood and sexual violence. One of the fundamental concerns that permeated the entire workshop was that, despite increased scrutiny of the role of religion in Australian sexual politics in recent years, the relationship between religion and sex in Australia was not well understood. This confusion was particularly evident in the context of sexual abuse in religious institutions. The Royal Commission, which is funded to run until the end of 2017, is contributing to this understanding as it explores the workings of various religious and secular organisations that have attempted to conceal their practices in relation to perpetrators. We hope that this volume will also make a significant contribution to international understandings of this vexed and sensitive 'wicked problem'.

The articles in this Special Issue are written from a range of feminist disciplinary responses, including law, criminology, anthropology and history. Together, the articles

---

[9] Worth Carolyn personal correspondence 22 June 2015.

[10] As above.

provide important historical context for the current social and political interest in clerical sex crimes, examine political and legal avenues for redress for survivors of these crimes and critically examine the ways in which church cultures position clergy and clergy offenders in relation to victims.

The special issue is opened by Lewis McCabe, who provides an intimate window into the experience of abuse survivors. His autobiographical note, and poetry written in response to the abuse he experienced in a religious institution of 'care', offer powerful insights into the harms suffered by the many thousands of survivors of clerical sex crime. We are extremely privileged to be able to include this personal contribution. Following McCabe, a praxis note by historian Fiona Davis provides valuable background to recent state inquiries. Davis situates the present Australian Royal Commission in a genealogy of inquiries into child welfare in Australia and internationally.[11] In particular, she highlights improvements in the position of survivors of abuse in state inquiries, and the ongoing problems with enacting the recommendations of such inquiries.

Kate Gleeson and Aleardo Zanghellini examine both church doctrines and innovative secular responses to crime as they scrutinise advocacy of Catholic Church-run restorative justice programs for clerical child sexual abuse.[12] Arguments for restorative justice in this context are sometimes grounded in the characterisation of the practice as an inherently Christian enterprise premised on 'grace', which may at first appear consistent with generalist restorative justice scholarship and processes emphasising the healing potential of forgiveness for victims. However, as the authors show, the Catholic doctrine of grace requires the pre-eminence of a goal not always explicitly emphasised by restorative justice advocates, namely, the rehabilitation — not only societal, but also spiritual — of the offender. Hence any Catholic restorative justice program centred on 'grace' has the potential for turning into an extraordinary demand made of victims not only to rehabilitate offenders and the Church in the eyes of the community, but also to work towards the spiritual absolution of the abuser. This feature of Catholic doctrine raises important concerns in terms of feminist critiques of the risk of gendered abuses of power within restorative justice, and is also incompatible with orthodox restorative justice theory, which, although it advocates a 'spiritual' response to crime, is concerned foremost with the rights, needs and experiences of victims.

Timothy Willem Jones investigates the historical articulation of clerical child sex crime in the canon law and informal governance practices of the Roman Catholic Church (1917–2001) and the Church of England (1870–1970).[13] Jones demonstrates that both churches have had longstanding practices for the discipline, surveillance and rehabilitation of clerical sex offenders. This history complicates established narratives in feminist history and the history of sexuality of the 'late discovery' of child sexual abuse from the 1970s. Analysing the historical development of canon law and informal

[11] Lewis McCabe, 'Perhaps Some Writing: And a Record of my Age' (2015) 41(2) *Australian Feminist Law Journal* 207; Davis Fiona 'The Royal Commission into Institutional Responses to Child Sexual Abuse: Learning from the Past' (2015) 41(2) *Australian Feminist Law Journal* 213.

[12] Gleeson Kate and Zanghellini Aleardo 'Graceful Remedies: Understanding Grace in the Catholic Church's Treatment of Clerical Child Sexual Abuse' (2015) 41(2) *Australian Feminist Law Journal* 219.

[13] Jones Timothy Willem 'Sin, Silence and States of Denial: Canon Law and the "Discovery" of Child Sexual Abuse' (2015) 41(2) *Australian Feminist Law Journal* 237.

governance practices in the light of Stanley Cohen' s late work on 'States of Denial' and feminist responses to 'archival silence', the article reveals techniques of denial through which, despite the explicit criminalisation of child sex offences in canon law, religious institutions were able to maintain silence around clerical sex offending.

Kim Stevenson, Judith Rowbotham and Jason Lowther examine avenues for remedies for clerical sex offences in the courts of the United Kingdom.[14] The authors document the recent flexibility of judgments holding churches to account as the courts, influenced by feminist critiques of law and the heightened profile of survivors, grapple with the public policy implications of torts of vicarious liability involving churches. Nonetheless, the authors argue that as a remedy for institutional sexual abuse, tort is constrained by inherent limitations related to both the institutional and financial organisation of churches, and the restorative function of awards. Financial recompense, when awarded, does not represent adequate reparation for clerical child sexual abuse, which warrants public acknowledgment of harm and apology. Redress through the courts must continue to evolve to represent the feminist principles of equality and responsibility before the law.

Meredith Edelman continues these themes to address, from a feminist intersectional standpoint, the limitations of litigation for clerical child sex offences in the USA.[15] Edelman identifies the numerous intersecting identities and characteristics of survivors of clerical child sexual abuse, which are often obscured or overlooked in mainstream profiles of individual survivors dominating the most well-publicised instances of mass and individual litigation. Focusing on the identity and social class of complainants, Edelman compares high-profile class actions in the US with less well-known bankruptcy suits, as means to provide survivors compensation. In instances where complainants appear financially and socially disempowered, bankruptcy has provided an unexpected path to compensation which may have significant restorative benefits for mass complainants, when compared to litigation.

Finally, Shurlee Swain analyses the impact of historical feminist discourses around child sexual abuse in enabling victims of institutional abuse to find a language in which to reconceptualise their experiences in out-of-home care.[16] Feminist articulations of sexual violence and sexual victimisation from the 1970s have allowed survivors to discredit the attitudes that prevailed during their childhood that looked-after children were morally inferior, and that the predominantly religious organisations that had responsibility for their care were above reproach, an attitude which simultaneously exposed such children to greater risks because of the lack of official oversight and discredited attempts they made to bring attention to their abuse. While the language of victimhood may come at a price it has given care leavers in Australia and beyond a powerful position from which to capture the attention of governments, to narrate their experiences of abuse and assert claims for redress.

[14] Stevenson Kim, Rowbotham Judith and Lowther Jason 'Reparation for Betrayal of Trust in Child Sexual Abuse Cases: The Christian Duty of Care, Vicarious Liability and the Church of England' (2015) 41(2) *Australian Feminist Law Journal* 253.
[15] Edelman Meredith 'An Unexpected Path: Bankruptcy, Justice and Intersecting Identities in the Catholic Sexual Abuse Scandals' (2015) 41(2) *Australian Feminist Law Journal* 271.
[16] Swain Shurlee 'Giving Voice to Narratives of Institutional Sex Abuse' (2105) 41(2) *Australian Feminist Law Journal* 289.

'Perhaps Some Writing: And a Record of my Age'

Lewis McCabe

Just a kid I was made a ward of state. The state removed me from my family and took on my 'care and protection'. In my 'best interests' I was sent to a Christian Boys' Home and while I was there I was subjected to emotional and physical abuse. Looking back on it I can see calling it a 'home' is a cruel joke. Home is a place of safety and love.

I experienced TOTAL loss of all control over my life. I was also powerless as I witnessed the abuse that other boys were subjected to. In the years since I have struggled with the aftermath of that childhood incarceration. Most importantly is my inability to trust.

In the 'home' I was groomed by an older male, a man of authority in the institution. He singled me out for attention, telling me I could be his 'top boy', and showing an interest in the poetry I wrote. This 'special treatment' was a relief from the general culture of abuse and denial. I was sucked in by his lies.

During my time in the home my father had a massive car accident, 'died' three times and was in the Intensive Care Unit at Royal Melbourne Hospital. The head screw, (who I did not realise was grooming me), told me truthfully that my father was 'about to die'. He misled me though, saying I would be picked up and taken to the hospital by a relative. When the relative arrived the head screw had knocked off work and had not left his authority for my release. This must have been deliberate, to demonstrate his power over me. Without his authorisation I was not given permission to leave the security yard. At this time I had no idea the head screw lived on the property and could easily have been contacted. At the first opportunity I did a runner and headed for the city to see dad. Against expectations dad survived his injuries. I wrote this poem:

Number 6

... I am number 6
In their book of tricks
And I'm ready packed to go
The route is set
And the liar's met
A more poisonous tongue than his
See, I'm not the average run o' the mill
Kid, who — dressed to kill —
Is out for blood, sex and fun
At the price of painful persuasion
I'm a more angry one.
(1978)[1]

Though I was an escapee for two days I knew on return I would be punished. Boss Harry, a large, dapper gentleman, advised me that: 'We know you had a reason, for stalling[2] but it is the lowest common denominator here and Justice MUST be seen to be done. Forty-Eight in the slot. Light on or light off?'.

If a boy broke the rules he could be confined in the 'slot'. This space was an old concrete toilet block with the ceramic bowls removed leaving a number of small concrete rooms the shape of a toilet with heavy wooden doors. We were placed in solitary there with a plastic bucket for pissing and shitting. (Minimal) food was passed through a flap in the bottom of the wooden door. The only option during the days of confinement was 'lights on the whole time or lights off'.

The next boy in the slot, caught playing chook footy[3] in the henhouse, was tasked with removing my graffiti, the poem 'Time', from the wall of the slot. This ended our friendship, such as it was.

Time

I have learned time is nothing
But this men made obstacle
I reap what I sow
Am here till let go
Never knowing why

[1] McCabe Lewis 'Number 6' unpublished poem 1978. Editorial Note: author aged 16.
[2] Editorial Note: 'Stalling' is a term used for people who absconded from the Home. Once they were returned they had only 'stalled' their time and had to see the original time of incarceration completed. Indeed in many cases they had to spend extra time locked up as punishment.
[3] Editorial Note: 'chook footy' was the term used for the activity at the Home where hens were kicked in the air towards hooks on the wall designated as goal posts.

All I miss is sunshine
48 in the slot.
(March 1978)[4]

I found the solitary confinement barbaric. However some of the boys showed great courage in smuggling me, through the door slot, cigarettes and porno mags that I never knew existed. This so-called discipline in solitary added a further layer of damage as I was developing my identity as an adolescent. This is the 'home' the state and the Christian institution used to rescue me.

The abuse that is the hardest to confront and talk about is the sexual abuse I suffered at the hands of the man who had groomed me. He encouraged me to drink alcohol, even taking me to a local pub and buying me drinks. This was illegal as I was underage and confined in his care as a ward of state. He abused me on the premises of the Christian home. Vivid flashbacks take me back to that place of horror often, especially during afternoons.

I dealt with the abuse by resorting to heavy drinking, substance abuse and working seven days a week in a physically demanding job. I needed to escape from my body. The concept of self-care has been absent from my life and my choices over and over have been self-destructive ones. I find my life is chaotic. I can't go to bed without lengthy rituals to secure the premises. I hide my wallet, keys, phone and so on so carefully that I can no longer find them when I wake.

The Dungeon

In the dungeon, I live everyday
In the dungeon, I go from 'A' to 'B'
This dungeon is a very big place
You see this dungeon and
You're in it with me

In the dungeon, there's another
It's specialised of course
I come from there, and with a beer
I dampen all my thoughts
It was a knackery
I'm a bi-producted horse

In the dungeon
If you don't blend in
They even stamp your shadow — VOID.[5]

My marriage broke down as a direct result of the damage I suffered while in the care of the Boys' Home and my inability to face that damage and seek treatment. My health has been affected by my alcoholism and failure in general to care for myself.

---

[4] McCabe Lewis 'Time' unpublished poem March 1978. Editorial Note: author aged 16.
[5] McCabe Lewis 'The Dungeon' unpublished poem 1980. Editorial Note: author aged 18.

Look

Look at me now
A thousand dreams wasted
Look at me now
Another day — I can't face it
And when I drink
I see truth
And when I cry I believe it
And if I tell you about it
It's only a modified version
I'm sorry I can't be tapped.[6]

I decided to speak out about my abuse in the hope that the people in authority with access to vulnerable children can be stopped from damaging other young people. In my Catholic convent school I was taught to respect church authority and believed that church officials were doing 'God's work'. The beatings, rapes and emotional lacerations meted out to boys in the Christian institution have turned my trust to shite.

I am a claimant, working with a legal team that is bringing a class action against the Boys' Home. The law moves slowly and requires evidence at every stage. Being part of the action requires lots of patience. It calls for stamina and discipline and the drive to do what I can to stop the abusers damaging other young lives. I realise that the law cannot bring justice, but it offers victims the chance to speak their truth.

Today I am in therapy and making an effort to face the reality of my abuse. I would like to confront my abuser. He may be regarded as a good Christian and respected in the community.

In truth: He is a criminal. He caused me pain. He caused me shame and humiliation. He betrayed my trust. He shattered my childhood. I do not know how I would react if I were to come face to face with him. I feel anger when I imagine such a meeting. I cannot imagine a healing of the deep places that were violated; the parts of me that he used for his pleasure. And he did not only offend against me; whatever is done to harm a child is an offence against us all.

Caged

I can paint a picture
Any way I please
Perfect, pathetic, perverted
It is all part
Of the same scheme
That ends as
Painfully peaceful
As the visions we receive of love —
Nailed to the heart of a dove

[6] Lewis McCabe, Look, 1980, unpublished poem. Editorial Note: author aged 18.

I can crush innocence
It is unreal
And only a phase
There is nothing that never
Knows the dark
Just someone who
Knows it too late.[7]

The Dark

Triumphant, confident confidante
Is always content to wait
I can never see the bottom
Of the beer
In its compact canister
What it does I can't control
But soon it doesn't matter
Smiling sinister is this amber
That releases me into a cage
For reasons unknown to myself
I know I will
Die in a fit of rage
And all that will be left
All I see to date, is my mistakes
(Perhaps some writing)
And a record of my age
And with these they can paint
Many varied pictures
While I rot in my final cage.
(1980)[8]

---

[7] McCabe Lewis 'Caged' unpublished poem 1980. Editorial Note: author aged 18.
[8] McCabe Lewis 'The Dark' unpublished poem 1980. Editorial Note: author aged 18. The author no longer believes that he 'will die in a fit of rage'. This poem was written soon after the abuse and reflects the anger arising from the powerlessness he felt.

The Royal Commission into Institutional Responses to Child Sexual Abuse: Learning from the Past

Fiona Davis

In the late 1890s a Royal Commission was held into the abuse of girls within a Sydney institute for the blind. Extraordinarily, from today's standpoint, the women testifying about their girlhood abuse at the hands of a teacher were cross-examined aggressively by the very man they were accusing.[1] More than 115 years later, the treatment of abuse survivors testifying at another inquiry into institutional child sexual abuse has been markedly different. While the potential for cross examination still stands, witnesses testifying before the Australian Royal Commission into Institutional Responses to Child Sexual Abuse ('Royal Commission') have been treated with considerably more care. At a hearing in May 2015 in Ballarat, for instance, a lawyer representing various arms of the Catholic Church, Peter Gray, stated he was unlikely to question survivors, even where their memories differed from those of church representatives. 'The church parties see these hearings primarily as an opportunity to listen to the witnesses and to truly hear what they say', Gray claimed.[2] Yet the current Royal Commission has not been without its challenges. This note takes an historical perspective to situate the current Royal Commission in a longer history of Australian child abuse inquiries. It also highlights some of the institutional and governmental responses to its work to date and the difficulties the Commissioners face with government enactment of their recommendations.

The Royal Commission was not the first governmental investigation of Australian institutions providing out-of-home 'care' to children. Shurlee Swain has identified 83 such inquiries, held between 1852 and 2013. Yet only since the 1990s have such investigations privileged survivor testimonies.[3] These more recent inquiries have been informed by the language of second-wave feminism, which recast

---

[1] Colony of New South Wales, Royal Commission of Inquiry into the Institution for the Blind Report of the Royal Commission Together with Appendix and Minutes of Evidence (1897 – 1898) in the State Records of New South Wales Series 1446 [4/993].

[2] Transcript of Proceedings, *Royal Commission into Institutional Responses to Child Sexual Abuse* (Ballarat Magistrates' Court, Public Hearing – Case Study 28, Day C77, 19 May 2015) at C8166. Available at: <http://www.childabuseroyalcommission.gov.au/case-study/860eabc6-e0fc-453a-b9d4-51a89852fede/case-study-28,-may-and-november-2015> Accessed 16 October 2015.

[3] Swain Shurlee *History of Inquiries Reviewing Institutions Providing Care for Children* Royal Commission into Institutional Responses to Child Sexual Abuse Sydney 2014 p 3 at 5–6.

'behaviours previously seen as the acts of individual "perverts" or "sex fiends"... as systemic'.[4] Drawing on this language, many survivors of abuse have been able to publically articulate their experiences.

The Royal Commission is part of an international movement of governmental inquiries into child abuse that began in the 1990s, inspired by truth commissions into human rights abuses, such as the South African Truth and Reconciliation Commission (1995–2002).[5] In 1999, Ireland established what would become a ten-year Commission to Inquire into Child Abuse in state-funded religious institutions between 1914 and 2000.[6] Since then many countries have investigated out-of-home abuse and neglect of children, including Finland, Sweden, Norway, Iceland, Denmark, Ireland, Northern Ireland, Wales and Scotland.[7]

Two critical senate inquiries in Australia investigated child abuse, one into the treatment of child migrants (2001) and the other into children in institutional 'care' (2004).[8] The latter, *Forgotten Australians*, estimated that in the previous 100 years more than 500,000 Australians had experienced out-of-home 'care'. Many reported traumatic experiences of abuse. A public campaign to investigate this abuse led by advocacy groups such as Bravehearts and the Care Leavers Australia Network (CLAN) gained significant media coverage.[9] In response, Victoria and New South Wales instituted inquiries in late 2012.[10] Shortly after, then Prime Minister Julia Gillard announced the Royal Commission, one of the few national inquiries to investigate institutions of all varieties, although its scope was limited to sexual abuse rather than abuse and mistreatment more broadly. Described as the 'gold standard' by Gerald Craddock in the Canadian context, Royal Commissions deliver greater powers of investigation than other inquiry formats in Australia and alternative international inquiry formats such as truth and reconciliation commissions.[11] In Australia, governed by the *Royal Commissions Act 1902*, they have 'special and coercive powers of investigation to collect and procure information,

[4] As above at 11.

[5] Sköld Johanna 'Apology Politics: Transnational Features' in Sköld Johanna and Swain Shurlee (eds) *Apologies and the Legacy of Abuse of Children in 'Care'* Palgrave Macmillan Basingstoke 2015 p 13 at 15.

[6] As above at 17.

[7] As above at 13.

[8] Commonwealth Senate, Community Affairs References Committee *Lost Innocents: Righting the record report on child migration* (2001); Commonwealth Senate, Community Affairs References Committee *Forgotten Australians: A report on Australians who experienced institutional or out-of-home care as children* (2004).

[9] Budiselik William, Crawford Frances and Chung Donna 'The Australian Royal Commission into Institutional Responses to Child Sexual Abuse: Dreaming of Child Safe Organisations?' (2014) 3 *Social Sciences* 565 at 567. See also Care Leavers of Australia Network (CLAN) 'Clan Postcard "Royal Commission into Child Sexual Abuse"' (2012) Available at: <http://www.findandconnect.gov.au/ref/australia/objects/FD0000017.htm> Accessed 16 October 2015.

[10] Middleton Warwick et al 'The Australian Royal Commission into Institutional Responses to Child Sexual Abuse' (2014) 48 *Australian & New Zealand Journal of Psychiatry* 17 at 17.

[11] Craddock Gerald 'Canadian Inquiries Stumble Towards Redress' in Sköld Johanna and Swain Shurlee (eds) *Apologies and the Legacy of Abuse of Children in 'Care'* Palgrave Macmillan Basingstoke 2015 p 134 at 135.

protect witnesses, compel witnesses to attend hearings and give evidence, even if self-incriminating'.[12]

The then Governor General Quentin Bryce declared the Royal Commission's formal appointment on 11 January 2013.[13] The Letters Patent, which set out the Terms of Reference, gave the Commissioners broad powers to investigate how to prevent future child sex abuse within institutions, identify best practice reporting procedures and propose schemes for the redress of historical abuses. Under Commission Chair Peter McClellan, the Commissioners were to consider strategies to improve responses to past and future abuse, with their recommendations extending to 'policy, legislative, administrative and structural reform'.[14] Survivor involvement was to be prioritised, with the Commissioners directed to provide 'opportunities for them to share their experiences in appropriate ways while recognising that many of them will be severely traumatised or will have special support needs'.[15] The Commissioners were not compelled to investigate any particular matter, so long as it was being 'appropriately dealt with by another inquiry or investigation or a criminal or civil proceeding'.[16] They could consider any institutions — private, public or non-government — that were currently or had previously been involved with children. The Commission was given until 31 December 2015 to complete its work, with a budget allocation from the government of AU$285 million.[17]

The Royal Commission has since undertaken a large-scale investigation through three main approaches: private sessions, public hearings and research and policy.[18] It has released one interim report, eight issues papers ranging from police responses to possible redress schemes, many research reports and has begun 33 case studies.[19] The Commissioners have held public hearings for 31 of the case studies and have reported on 14. The traumatic experiences of abuse heard at the hearings have been widely reported.[20] Despite concerns that survivors may be re-traumatised by sharing their stories, many have reported positively on the experience.[21] The historic

[12] Prasser Scott 'Royal Commissions in Australia: When Should Governments Appoint Them?' (2006) 65 *Australian Journal of Public Administration* 28 at 32.
[13] Royal Commission into Institutional Responses to Child Sexual Abuse (Commonwealth) *Letters Patent* (2013). Available at: <http://www.childabuseroyalcommission.gov.au/about-us/terms-of-reference> Accessed 16 October 2015.
[14] As above.
[15] As above.
[16] As above.
[17] Royal Commission into Institutional Responses to Child Sexual Abuse (Commonwealth) *Interim Report Volume 1* (2014) 2, 35.
[18] As above at 1.
[19] Royal Commission into Institutional Responses to Child Sexual Abuse, Available at: <http://www.childabuseroyalcommission.gov.au/> Accessed 16 October 2015.
[20] See McFadyen Warwick 'Sex Abuse Inquiry: How Evil Stole the Innocence of Children' *Brisbane Times* 24 May 2015 <http://www.brisbanetimes.com.au/comment/sex-abuse-inquiry-how-evil-stole-the-innocence-of-children-20150523-gh6h0a.html> Accessed 19 July 2015; King Austin 'Witness Retells Harrowing Experience at Neerkol Orphanage' *The Morning Bulletin* 14 April 2015 <http://www.themorningbulletin.com.au/news/spotlight-on-dark-past-of-orphanage/2605946> Accessed 19 July 2015.
[21] See King Austin 'Neerkol Victim Fulfils Mum's Dying Wish' *The Morning Bulletin* 17 April 2015 <http://www.themorningbulletin.com.au/news/david-fulfils-mums-dying-wish/2609977> Accessed 19 July 2015.

institutional responses to abuse allegations investigated by the inquiry have been universally found wanting.[22] Given the scale of the Royal Commission's preliminary findings, the Commissioners requested a two-year extension, which the government granted in September 2014, bringing the total budget for the inquiry to just over AU$500 million.[23] Even with the revised 15 December 2017 deadline, McClellan flagged in early July 2015 that the Commission would struggle to hear from everyone seeking to share their story.[24] At that time, the Commission had already received over 23,500 telephone calls, almost 12,000 letters and emails and just over 3,700 private sessions.[25]

Many institutions have responded swiftly and decisively following investigation by the Royal Commission. By June 2015, all board members of the Yeshiva Centre in Melbourne had stepped down following a two-week hearing in February 2015 into responses to allegations of child sexual abuse at the Centre.[26] Also in June, the Anglican diocese in Wangaratta became the third Victorian Anglican diocese to become a company so child abuse survivors could more easily sue for redress.[27] In July 2015, the Christian Brothers resettled with abuse survivors in Western Australia following a review prompted by the Commission.[28]

Not all religious institutions have been as accommodating. Former Archbishop of Sydney Cardinal George Pell's testimony in August 2014, delivered remotely from the Vatican, compared the church's responsibility for its clergy's sexual offences to that of a trucking company for offences committed by its drivers.[29] In that same hearing Pell also stated that it was not appropriate for the Vatican to hand over all documents

---

[22] See AAP 'Melb Children's Hospital in Abuse Inquiry' *The Australian* 7 May 2015 <http://www.theaustralian.com.au/news/latest-news/melb-childrens-hospital-in-abuse-inquiry/story-fn3dxiwe-1227338904297> Accessed 20 July 2015; Collins Antonette 'Scott Volkers Allegations' *ABC Online* 8 July 2014 <http://www.abc.net.au/news/2014-07-08/royal-commission-child-sexual-abuse-scott-volkers/5581492> Accessed 19 July 2015.

[23] Attorney-General for Australia 'Transcript: Extension of Royal Commission into Institutional Responses to Child Sexual Abuse' 2 September 2013, available at <http://www.attorneygeneral.gov.au/transcripts/Pages/2014/ThirdQuarter2014/2September2014-ExtensionofRoyalCommissionintoInstitutionalResponsestoChildSexualAbuse.aspx> Accessed 16 October 2015.

[24] AAP 'Royal Commission Running out of Time' *The Guardian* 4 July 2015 <http://www.theguardian.com/australia-news/2015/jul/04/royal-commission-running-out-of-time-to-hear-child-sex-abuse-victims> Accessed 19 July 2015.

[25] Royal Commission into Institutional Responses to Child Sexual Abuse, Available at: <http://www.childabuseroyalcommission.gov.au/> Accessed 16 October 2015.

[26] Jacks Timna 'Yeshiva Centre's Leadership Dissolved in Wake of Abuse Revelations' *The Age* (Melbourne) 17 June 2015 <http://www.theage.com.au/victoria/yeshivah-centres-leadership-dissolved-in-wake-of-abuse-revelations-20150617-ghpclb.html> Accessed 29 July 2015.

[27] AAP 'Vic Churches to Become "Companies" so Child Abuse Victims Can Sue' *SBS News* 10 June 2015 <http://www.sbs.com.au/news/article/2015/06/10/vic-churches-become-companies-so-child-abuse-victims-can-sue> Accessed 29 July 2015.

[28] Nicholson Leanne 'Christian Brothers Resettle with WA Abuse Victims after Royal Commission Review' *WAtoday* 7 July 2015 <http://www.watoday.com.au/wa-news/christian-brothers-resettle-with-wa-abuse-victims-after-royal-commission-review-20150706-gi68uu.html> Accessed 29 July 2015.

[29] Lee Jane and Houston Cameron 'Pell Compares Priests to Truckers as Victims Given Apologies' *Sydney Morning Herald* 22 August 2014 <http://www.smh.com.au/federal-politics/political-news/pell-compares-priests-to-truckers-as-victims-given-apologies-20140821-3e3mk.html#ixzz3gbPhAxzi> Accessed 29 July 2015.

relevant to child sex abuse by priests in Australia. Pell's observation followed a refusal by the Vatican to do just this when the Commission applied to it in writing earlier that year.[30] This general reluctance to comply with document requests continued in mid-July 2015, when the Church's insurance company was given a week to produce close to 2000 files, after failing to meet an earlier deadline to produce these documents.[31]

Current Prime Minister Malcolm Turnbull, as did his predecessor Tony Abbott, appeared sympathetic to the Royal Commission. In March 2015, however, the government advised the Commission not to pursue a Commonwealth-funded national redress scheme for abuse survivors — an option discussed in a Commission consultation paper two months earlier. That paper noted that survivors preferred such a model.[32] In a written submission the Federal Government instead suggested that the Royal Commission 'make recommendations that institutions must accept the legal, financial and moral responsibility for failing to protect children'. [33] McClellan voiced the Commission's disappointment, given that such a scheme was 'overwhelmingly supported by survivor advocacy and support groups and by many institutions'.[34] Catholic Church Truth Justice and Healing Council CEO Francis Sullivan was similarly critical noting 'It's surprising to say the least that the Government initiated the call to the royal commission and yet [it] has so quickly discounted itself from one of the fundamental issues we have to address'.[35] He said independence was essential to the future compensation of survivors: 'The days of the Church doing its own investigations are over'.[36] The Commission's proposed investigation of child sexual abuse in Australia's immigration detention centres will likely have further implications for the Royal Commission's relationship with the Federal Government.[37]

Taken from a historical perspective, the Royal Commission has many advantages over past inquiries into institutional child sexual abuse, particularly with regard to its

[30] Gilmore Heath 'Vatican Rebuffs Justice Peter McClellan on Sex Abuse Files' *Sydney Morning Herald* 6 July 2015 <http://www.smh.com.au/national/vatican-rebuffs-justice-peter-mcclellan-on-sex-abuse-files-20140705-3bf51.html> Accessed 30 July 2015.

[31] Lavoipierre Angela 'Child Sex Abuse Royal Commission: Catholic Church Insurance Group Given Week to Produce 2,000 Documents' *The World Today ABC* <http://www.abc.net.au/news/2015-07-10/catholic-church-insurance-group-given-week-to-produce-files/6610640> Accessed 29 July 2015.

[32] Royal Commission into Institutional Responses to Child Sexual Abuse (Commonwealth) *Consultation Paper: Redress and Civil Litigation* (2015) 55–56.

[33] Kidd Jessica 'Child Sex Abuse Royal Commission: Victims Condemn Federal Government Opposition to National Support Scheme, Referral of Responsibility to Institutions' 26 March 2015 *ABC Online* <http://www.abc.net.au/news/2015-03-25/commonwealth-doesnt-back-national-support-scheme-abuse-victims/6346102> Accessed 29 July 2015.

[34] Cited in Brereton Adam 'Child Abuse Victims Deserve More Than the Commonwealth's Excuses' *The Guardian* 26 March 2015 <http://www.theguardian.com/commentisfree/2015/mar/26/child-abuse-victims-deserve-more-than-the-commonwealths-excuses> Accessed 19 July 2015.

[35] Cited in Kidd Jessica 'Child Sex Abuse Royal Commission: Catholic Church Says Rejection of National Compensation and Support Scheme Surprising' 26 March 2015 <http://www.abc.net.au/news/2015-03-26/rejection-national-scheme-support-child-abuse-victims-surprising/6349940> Accessed 29 July 2015.

[36] As above.

[37] Australian Human Rights Commission *The Forgotten Children: National Inquiry into Children in Immigration Detention* (2014) 62.

powers and its scope. To date it has used these advantages wisely, reflecting advances in inquiry practices, particularly the prioritisation of survivor voices. Many institutions have already responded with changes, although others have resisted investigation. The Commission's relationship with the Federal Government is imperfect, however, and it may face challenges with regard to the implementation of its recommendations, particularly in light of the recent national redress scheme controversy. Yet, writing today in July 2015, the Commission still has the potential to become the 'enduring global benchmark' hoped for by Warwick Middleton et al.[38] The Independent Inquiry into Child Sexual Abuse in England and Wales, which commenced on 9 July 2015, is looking to the Australian example.[39] Where some past inquiries may have faded into obscurity, this Commission has the potential to instigate lasting changes to the ways that institutions and wider society responds to allegations of child sexual abuse.

[38] Middleton above note 10 at 27.

[39] Independent Inquiry into Child Sexual Abuse (IICSA) 'Background' Available at: <https://www.iicsa.org.uk/about-the-inquiry/background> Accessed 16 October 2015.

Graceful Remedies: Understanding Grace in the Catholic Church's Treatment of Clerical Child Sexual Abuse

Kate Gleeson and Aleardo Zanghellini

Abstract. This article examines advocacy of Catholic restorative justice for clerical child sexual abuse from the standpoint of feminist criminological critiques of the use of restorative mediation in sexual offence cases. In particular, it questions the Catholic invocation of grace and forgiveness of survivors of abuse in light of critical feminist concerns about the exploitation of emotions in restorative practices, especially in regard to sexual and other gender-based offences. In the context of sexual abuse, the Catholic appeal to grace has the potential for turning into an extraordinary demand made of victims not only to rehabilitate offenders and the Church in the eyes of the community, but also to work towards the spiritual absolution of the abuser. This unique feature of Catholic-oriented restorative justice raises important concerns in terms of feminist critiques of the risk of abuses of power within mediation, and is also incompatible with orthodox restorative justice theory, which, although it advocates a 'spiritual' response to crime, is concerned foremost with the rights, needs and experiences of victims.

1.0 Introduction

The international crisis of revelations of enduring and systemic abuse in Catholic (and other) institutions has led some scholars, practitioners and churches to advocate restorative justice as a remedy for historical child sexual abuse perpetrated by clergy and other church personnel. Advocacy of restorative justice in this context is based on the unique harms of clerical child sexual abuse, which devastate spiritual, interpersonal and communal relationships. Arguments for the healing of such relationships via restorative justice are grounded in the characterisation of the practice as an inherently Christian enterprise premised on 'grace', which may at first appear consistent with generalist restorative justice scholarship and processes emphasising the healing potential of forgiveness for the victims, or survivors, of abuse.[1] 'Grace', however, has a unique meaning in Catholic thought and is arguably distinct from secular understandings of the concept. In this article we provide a theoretical discussion of the Catholic doctrine of grace to explain what it would mean to apply this doctrine in the context of restorative justice in cases of historical clerical child sexual abuse. We do so in light of critical feminist criminological concerns about the exploitation of emotions such as forgiveness in restorative practices, especially with regard to sexual and other gender-based offences.

'Grace' in the Catholic context is not simply an invocation of goodwill; the forgiveness that Catholic 'grace' suggests is not simply an appeal to victims to reconcile relationships with perpetrators. Rather, an analysis of the doctrine of grace with regard to crime suggests that grace is concerned with the Church's performance of good offices on behalf of *the perpetrator* to rehabilitate him in the eyes of God and to induce, in support of this goal, the forgiveness of those whose bodily and psychosexual boundaries he has transgressed. As we will show, the grace of God is, first and foremost, what the perpetrator of the abuse has *lost* in committing abuse. Grace is also, however, what can be *wished upon him*, as it were, by the victim. In Catholic thought, the victim of a crime has the power to invoke 'actual graces' (Godly gifts) that will help the perpetrator of that crime recover the full grace of God, which will in turn cleanse him of sin and save his soul.

Thus, in the context of restorative justice and sexual abuse, we suggest that a Catholic appeal to grace has the potential for turning into an extraordinary demand made of victims not only to rehabilitate offenders and the Church in the eyes of the community, but also to work towards the spiritual absolution of the abuser. This feature of Catholic doctrine raises important concerns in terms of feminist critiques of the risk of gendered abuses of power within mediation, and is also incompatible with orthodox restorative justice theory, which, although it advocates a 'spiritual' response to crime, is concerned foremost with the rights, needs and experiences of victims.

We begin by briefly outlining the conventional understanding of restorative justice, which makes redress of harm to victims its central goal, and we discuss feminist concerns that restorative justice may fail to deliver on this goal in the context of sexual crime, especially in its focus on forgiveness and the reconciliation of relationships. We then clarify the special nature of Christian advocacy for restorative justice, which is centred on the concepts of forgiveness and grace, and demonstrate the recent trend in advocating and implementing church-run restorative justice schemes for child sexual abuse in this context. We examine the goals of these schemes as stated by their advocates and explain how the Catholic doctrine of

[1] We note here that we are sensitive to the need for victims of abuse to reclaim the loss of subjectivity, control and empowerment denoted by the term 'victim' through the alternative use of the word 'survivor'; yet we must also acknowledge 'victim' and 'offender' as legal entities. This paper thus refers to people who have experienced abuse as 'victims' when we wish to emphasise their status as objects of violation by perpetrators, and as 'survivors' when we wish to place the emphasis instead on their subjective capacity for agency beyond the victim/offender dichotomy, or to indicate life lived beyond the initial instance/s of abuse.

grace requires the pre-eminence of a goal not always explicitly emphasised, namely, the rehabilitation — not only societal, but also spiritual — of the offender. Lastly, we show how this logic of Catholic grace all but requires the cooperation of the survivor of the abuse in this rehabilitation, through the act of forgiveness, and how this example gives particular force to feminist concerns about the emotionally exploitative potential of restorative justice in cases of sexual crime. We conclude by drawing attention to the epistemological discontinuities between calls for restorative justice centred on Catholic grace and orthodox (victim-centred) restorative justice, and we warn of the perils of theorists and practitioners uncritically appropriating theological terminology, especially in the context of very grave offences such as child sexual abuse.

2.0 Restorative Justice and Feminist Critiques

Restorative justice is a form of alternative dispute resolution offered as an adjunct to criminal justice, which aims to bring together all stakeholders affected by harm in a process distinct from traditional corrective justice, in which addressing the 'harm done to the victim takes precedence'.[2] Crime is viewed as a violation of human relationships, and the restorative process focuses on the restoration of those relationships, offering the 'reunion of the two individuals and of the individual with the community'[3] as a way of 'healing the hurts of injustice and transforming the conditions that allowed injustice to flourish'.[4] Typically, restorative justice is promoted in contrast to adversarial criminal justice, which is not victim-centred and 'effectively discourages truth telling and inadvertently discourages offenders from acknowledging responsibility for their crime'.[5]

Support for restorative justice in the context of sexual crime tends to reflect disenchantment with the criminal justice system, whereby despite 30 years of 'significant change' to responses to sexual violence, conviction rates have fallen in Australia, Canada, England, Wales and elsewhere.[6] For example, a 2014 Irish study (hereafter, the Irish Study) based on interviews with sex offenders, victims and other stakeholders concluded that due to the very high attrition rate for the criminal treatment of sexual offences, restorative justice programs should be trialled in Ireland.[7] Legal theorists such as Carol Smart and Nicola Lacey maintain that the failures of conventional criminal justice are not procedural, but intrinsic to the criminal law, which 'disqualifies' the

[2] Umbreit Mark and Armour Marilyn Peterson *Restorative Justice Dialogue: An Essential Guide for Research and Practice* Springer New York 2010 p 7.

[3] Gavrielides Theo 'Clergy Child Sexual Abuse and the Restorative Justice Dialogue' (2012) 55 *Journal of Church and State* 617–39.

[4] Braithwaite John *Restorative Justice and Responsive Regulation* Oxford University Press New York 2002 p 564.

[5] Keenan Marie *Sexual Trauma and Abuse: Restorative and Transformative Possibilities? A Collaborative Study on the Potential of Restorative Justice in Sexual Crime in* Ireland University College Dublin School of Applied Social Science Dublin 2014 p 21.

[6] Daly Kathleen 'Conventional and Innovative Justice Responses to Sexual Violence' (2011) 12 *ACSSA Issues* 1 at 1.

[7] Keenan above note 5.

harm of sexual violence.[8] In this context, Hudson writes of the discursive power of restorative justice to challenge stereotypical understandings of sexual victimisation, blame and responsibility.[9] Similarly, the authors of the Irish Study describe victims as desiring a 'rebalancing of the power dynamic' of sexual offences, which restorative justice may provide.[10]

While over the past two decades, restorative justice has been promoted as an answer, and in some cases '*the* answer'[11] to the failings of criminal justice, its use in cases of sexual violence and other gender-based harms remains the topic of 'vigorous' debate among criminologists and practitioners.[12] Feminist critiques of restorative practices have mostly been made theoretically, in the context of adult survivors of recently committed offences. There exist only a handful of studies appraising restorative justice programs delivered in the context of sexually violent offences, such as victim-offender mediation for juvenile offenders and prison inmates.[13] Restorative justice in the context of historical, institutional child sexual abuse is particularly under-studied. A 2011 Scottish pilot study of adult survivors of childhood abuse in care determined that restorative justice 'can be a positive remedy for some survivors' as it may help them 'deal with' the harm they suffered, and offenders to 'accept responsibility for this harm'.[14] However, New Zealand research found that survivors of historical child sexual abuse are reluctant to participate in restorative justice and that any targeted programs would need to accommodate their recovery processes and difficulties associated with disclosing abuse to family and friends.[15] Crucially, there exists no comparative analysis of historical sexual offences finalised in court and by restorative conferences.[16]

Some authors and practitioners warn that all forms of alternative dispute resolution risk 'domesticating stories of violence so they become stories of conflict'[17] by reframing victims' rights as needs and depoliticising gender-based harms by embodying the 'qualities of the private' in mediation.[18] In particular, Stubbs disputes the ability of restorative justice to remedy gender-based offences, which are not

---

[8] Smart Carol *Feminism and the Power of Law* Routledge London and New York 1989; Lacey Nicola 'Unspeakable subjects, Impossible rights: Sexuality, Integrity and Criminal Law' (1998) 11(1) *Canadian Journal of Law and Jurisprudence* 47–68.
[9] As above at 24.
[10] Keenan above note 5 at 173.
[11] Stubbs Julie 'Restorative Justice, Domestic Violence and Family Violence' (2004) *Domestic Violence and Family Violence Clearinghouse, Issues Paper 9* 1 (emphasis in original).
[12] Keenan Marie and Joyce Niamh *Restorative Justice and Sexual Violence: Ireland Joins the International Debate* University College Dublin School of Applied Social Science Dublin 2013 p 8.
[13] As above at 15; see also Daly Kathleen 'Restorative Justice and Sexual Assault: An Archival Study of Court and Conference Cases' (2006) 46 *British Journal of Criminology* 334.
[14] Survivor Scotland 2011 <http://www.survivorscotland.org.uk/confidential-forum/time-to-be-heard/restorative-justice-toolkit/>.
[15] Jülich Shirley 'Views of Justice Among Survivors of Historical Child Sexual Abuse: Implications for Restorative Justice in New Zealand' (2006) 10 *Theoretical Criminology* 125 at 136.
[16] Daly above note 6 at 23.
[17] Cobb Sara 'The Domestication of violence in Mediation' (1997) 31 *Law and Society Review* 397–440; Coker Donna 'Enhancing Autonomy for Battered Women: Lessons from Navajo Peacemaking' (1999) 47 *UCLA Law Review* 1–111.
[18] As above.

incident-based but repeated, often over many years, and are concerned with power and control.[19] Theorising crime as primarily a conflict between individuals fails to engage with questions of structural disadvantage and with systemic raced, classed and gendered patterns of crime.[20]

Of crucial concern to Stubbs is the role of *emotions* connected to remorse, apology and forgiveness in restorative practices, which Braithwaite identifies as the 'central focus' of the process:

> the objective is to get all the dimensions of how people feel into the circle so everyone in the circle can ask themselves if they can make any contribution to resolving those feelings.[21]

To succeed at providing a sense of justice, restorative justice requires offender remorse. However, gendered and sexual abuses tend to be characterised by power and control, the effects of which the offender is unlikely to appreciate.[22] Cossins suggests it is possible for offenders to apologise without remorse and for victims to feel distress during restorative processes,[23] as questions of forgiveness and grace loom large in their experiences. Although Braithwaite cautions it is 'cruel and wrong' to necessarily expect forgiveness,[24] restorative justice theory and practice does value forgiveness as healing and empowering for victims.[25] Hence, Stubbs warns of ethical challenges for mediators who may communicate expectations of apology and forgiveness and exploit gendered emotions in the pursuit of outcomes valued in restorative justice. Restorative justice advocates rarely engage adequately with questions of 'how gender, and other social relations, might be related to the construction of meaning within, and to the emotional dynamics of, restorative processes'.[26]

3.0 The Christian Approach to Restorative Justice

Feminist attention to the use of emotions in mediation is, ironically, mirrored in Christian advocacy of restorative justice, which promotes forgiveness and grace as the practice's most compelling and *therapeutic* features offering a form of transcendence for both victims and offenders. While many theorists associate the movement's key concepts with traditional indigenous cultures,[27] Christian advocates, including judges and other legal representatives, instead promote restorative practices as offering

---

[19] Stubbs above note 11 at 6.
[20] As above.
[21] Braithwaite above note 4 at 252.
[22] Stubbs above note 11 at 171.
[23] Cossins Anne 'Restorative Justice and Child Sex Offences: The Theory and the Practice' (2008) 48 *British Journal of Criminology* 359 at 362.
[24] Braithwaite above note 4 at 570–71.
[25] Zehr Howard *Changing Lenses. A New Focus for Crime and Justice* Herald Press Scottdale 2005 pp 49–52; Umbreit and Armour above note 2 at 74–5.
[26] Stubbs Julie 'Beyond Apology? Domestic Violence and Critical Questions for Restorative Justice' (2007) 7 *Criminology & Criminal Justice* 169 at 172.
[27] Armour and Umbreit 'Victim Forgiveness in Restorative Justice Dialogue' (2006) 1 *Victims and Offenders: An International Journal of Evidence-Based Research, Policy and Practice* 123 at 124.

redemption of offenders and the justice system as a whole, in terms of Judaeo-Christian biblical teachings. Some of the strongest advocacy of restorative justice emanates from Christians inspired by founding theorist Mennonite Christian Howard Zehr, who stresses the centrality of forgiveness to restorative approaches as something 'that must come in its own time with God's help'.[28] Christians characterise restorative justice as challenging the legal community to transform its focus from punishing offenders to 'inspiring grace in victims and offenders by showing compassion'.[29] In this argument, orthodox justice represents a failure of morality, spirituality and legal procedure. Crucially, justice hinges on the 'hard' emotional work of victims to forgive:

> While punitive justice does little to actually mend wrong, restorative justice in contrast is all about making things right, about changing negative dynamics and helping people to overcome hurt. That's what grace is all about: it does not ignore problems, but in fact addresses them on a much deeper level than punitive justice does. So while grace may be in conflict with a strictly punitive understanding of justice, it is not in conflict with restorative justice. In fact, grace is all about restorative justice. ... Grace is indeed hard, but even taking a few small faltering steps in its direction can open the doors for healing to start and violence to stop. That's why grace is not an ideal luxury, but quite literally a life and death necessity. Grace is the very means by which true justice comes about.[30]

Even secular restorative justice theory sometimes emphasises the Christian roots and spiritual dimensions of the practices. Braithwaite cites St Paul that 'where sin abounded, grace did much more abound' and describes crime as an 'opportunity to prevent greater evils, to confront crime with a grace that transforms human lives to paths of love and giving'.[31] Grace he promotes as providing victims the 'spiritual restoration' required for healing.[32] However orthodox theorists such as Braithwaite tend not to explain what they understand or mean by theological concepts such as 'grace', or the essential implications of this 'spiritual' worldview for victims and offenders participating in mediation. Even Zehr appears to collapse the categories of 'forgiveness' and 'grace' as one and the same, despite the distinct theological meaning of the latter.[33] The uncritical promotion of Christian terminology in restorative justice scholarship has meant that increasingly such arguments have come to be applied to cases of clerical child sexual abuse, and have acquired distinctive connotations in the Catholic context, with its characteristic understanding of grace, mortal sin and salvation. The implications of this may not be appreciated by theorists and practitioners who unwittingly grant Catholic Church-run restorative justice programs authority.

---

[28] Zehr note 25 at 46.

[29] Grimes Diana 'Practice What You Preach: How Restorative Justice Could Solve the Judicial Problems in Clergy Sexual Abuse Cases' (2006) 63 *Washington and Lee Law Review* 1693 at 1703.

[30] Flood Derek 'Restorative Justice and the Economy of Grace' *Huffington Post* 20 October 2011 <http://www.huffingtonpost.com/derek-flood/restorative-justice-and-t_b_1016850.html>. Accessed 30 August 2015

[31] Braithwaite above note 4 at 3.

[32] As above at 46.

[33] Zehr above note 25 at 51.

4.0 Catholic Restorative Justice and Child Sexual Abuse

Following the 1990s' North American 'litigation explosion', which had been forewarned by the US Catholic hierarchy as 'the most serious crisis that we in the church have faced in centuries', numerous dioceses in Canada and the US filed for bankruptcy protections and sought means by which to settle sex abuse complaints out of court.[34] This included the development and delivery of in-house restorative justice programs facilitating mediation with adult survivors of church-based childhood abuses. Advocates of these programs link contemporary restorative justice values to those upheld by the church 'throughout history', such as by way of the Catholic confessional, which developed as a 'restorative approach to encourage personal responsibility and reconciliation with God'.[35] It is the teaching of the Church that punishment for a crime, 'in addition to defending public order and protecting people's safety, has a medicinal purpose: [a]s far as possible, it must contribute to the correction of the guilty party'.[36] Restorative justice is therefore promoted as a means compatible with the Catholic approach to crime for 'repairing harm by giving voice to the victims, restoring the community and rehabilitating offenders through responsibility and reconciliation',[37] with 'equal weight' given to the interests of the victims, the Church and perpetrators and the community.[38]

In the context of clerical child sexual abuse, restorative justice is promoted as being in the best interests of both victims and the Church. Mediation is promoted as best for victims, with arguments that orthodox justice fails to address their particular 'esoteric pathos',[39] while restorative justice is promoted as best for the Church in terms of its being:

> rooted in theology and the Christian themes of forgiveness and reconciliation [which] should make it particularly attractive to a Church craving reunion with its followers and a higher moral road not offered by the traditional justice system.[40]

Justified as such, restorative justice programs have come to be offered as a form of salvation for survivors and offenders in the US, New Zealand, Australia, the Netherlands and elsewhere.[41] This is despite the lack of significant robust research determining the suitability and efficacy of restorative justice for historical, institutional child sexual

[34] Jenkins Philip *Pedophiles and Priests: Anatomy of a Contemporary Crisis* Oxford University Press Oxford and New York 2001 p 37.
[35] Grimes above note 29 at 1703.
[36] Catechism of the Catholic Church no 2266.
[37] Catholic Mobilizing Network 2015 <http://catholicsmobilizing.org/8436/november-21-2014-conference-restorative-justice-washington-d-c/>. Accessed 30 August 2015
[38] Gavrielides Theo and Coker Dale. 'Restoring Faith: Resolving the Roman Catholic Church's Sexual Scandals Through Restorative Justice (Working Paper I)' (2005) 8 *Contemporary Justice Review* 345–65.
[39] As above at 355.
[40] As above at 363.
[41] As above. Chiste Katherine Beaty 'Faith-Based Organizations and the Pursuit of Restorative Justice' (2006) 32 *Manitoba Law Review* 27; Gleeson Kate 'The Money Problem: Reparation and Restorative Justice in the Catholic Church's Towards Healing Program' (2015) 26 *Current Issues in Criminal Justice* 317.

abuse noted above. Organisations such as the British Independent Academic Research Studies think tank have begun to document (and advocate for) existing programs.[42] International data are generally incoherent, however, as programs tend to operate beyond the shadow of the law and are individual to the communities and organisations that host them: 'there is no central registry. There is no one prototype. Information … is scattered and empirical'.[43] It is not apparent to what extent various church-led processes abide by restorative justice standards or provide a sense of justice for survivors and offenders.

Although representatives of the Vatican have made public statements that sex offenders should remain accountable through ordinary criminal justice processes, and orthodox restorative justice theory mandates that mediation only ever be offered as an *optional adjunct* to criminal processes, some Catholic advocates such as Grimes steer perilously close to advocating the undermining of established restorative justice standards, and the rule of law, when they suggest that the best way to 'break the cycle' is for 'the church and the offending priests to meet with the victims and settle the problems outside of the judicial system'.[44] Furthermore, significant evidence collated in government inquiries suggests, for example, that Australian Catholic Church-led processes fail to uphold general restorative justice standards aimed at protecting victims, and do not confront the specific feminist concerns about cases of sexual abuse, especially historical institutional child sexual abuse.[45]

5.0 Restoring Relationships: The Essence of Restorative Justice

Orthodox restorative justice theory aims to harness forgiveness and 'grace' to restore relationships, where possible, between victim, offender and community. Hence Catholic advocates argue that restorative justice may perform the function of restoring four unique relationships central to religious child sexual abuse. First among these is the relationship of survivors to their faith. Clerical child sex offences share common attributes with other child sex offences: calculated, premeditated grooming activities to gain sexual access to a child, with risks and benefits weighed up by perpetrators; repeated abuse escalating in gravity of offences; and significant time-lags in reporting, if ever,[46] with the criminal justice system experienced as 'extremely traumatic by victims and their families'.[47] Most, if not all, sexual abuse provokes 'potent and debilitating self-blame' among victims.[48] However, it is argued, along with the violation of a sacrosanct relationship that 'once embodied ultimate trust',[49] abuse by clergy constitutes the extra abusive dimension of the violation of an individual's basic human right to faith and identity, which may be experienced by Catholic religious victims

[42] Gavrielides above note 3.
[43] Beaty above note 41 at 29.
[44] Grimes above note 29 at 1695.
[45] Gleeson above note 41.
[46] Cossins above note 23 at 365.
[47] Keenan above note 5 at 30.
[48] As above at 20.
[49] Gavrielides and Coker above note 38 at 346.

as a 'sacrilege that offends against a sacramental worldview' that is central to Catholicism.[50]

Abuse by clergy results in significant trauma and distress related to 'theological belief, crises of faith, and fears about one's mortality'.[51] These are outcomes one Christian commentator described in terms of the 'murder of a person's soul',[52] which orthodox justice is not equipped to address. The spiritual nature of abuse brings with it particular individual harms akin to post-traumatic stress disorder with potentially lifelong effects and may also act as a significant deterrent for acknowledging and/or reporting abuse,[53] with concomitant harms that extend to the religious community, including the victim's family. Catholic restorative justice advocates argue that healing must attend to the religious challenges implied by the abuse, ideally through restorative mediation.

A second aim for Catholic advocates concerns the restoration of the survivor's relationship with, if not the individual perpetrator, then the Church as a whole. Complicity of the institution and religious hierarchy has frequently compounded effects of abuse for which the Church has been found morally and legally liable in numerous jurisdictions. While restorative justice has typically been theorised and implemented to address relationships between *individuals*, some authors optimistically advocate for its healing capacities to extend to the relationship between the individual and the *institution*.

A third aim concerns that of restoring the relationship of the Church with the religious community to allow, ideally, a diocese 'to stand proud before parishioners and others'.[54] Some Catholic respondents to the Irish Study noted the inability of the criminal justice system to perform this function, and identified non-complicit members of the Church, as well as congregations, as 'secondary victims' of perpetrators' abusive behaviours. Restorative justice was viewed as offering great potential for internal and external church reconciliation,[55] even though the process focuses on the experiences of individual victims.

Finally, is the aim of restoring the perpetrator's relationship with the Church, which we argue is the most pressing concern for considerations of the role of grace and emotion in restorative practices. Some Catholic religious leaders responding to the Irish Study noted that clerical offenders feel 'abandoned' by the Church as they progress through criminal or civil proceedings.[56] The respondents identified hypocrisy in this abandonment — 'You can't preach forgiveness and not give forgiveness' — and viewed restorative justice as potentially 'humanising' for offenders and allowing for reconciliation with their faith and the Church.[57] An analysis of the Catholic doctrine of grace explains why these respondents may

[50] Guido Joseph J 'A Unique Betrayal: Clergy Sexual Abuse in the Context of the Catholic Religious Tradition' (2008) 17 *Journal of Child Sexual Abuse* 255 at 260.
[51] Gavrielides above note 3 at 620.
[52] As above at 620.
[53] As above.
[54] Gavrielides above note 3 at 627.
[55] Keenan above note 5 at 290–1.
[56] As above.
[57] As above.

have viewed Catholic restorative justice as capable of restoring perpetrators not only to the Church, but to God Himself. We turn to this analysis in the next section, arguing that in most cases the logic of Catholic grace all but *requires* that Catholic approaches to restorative justice invoking grace make the offender's salvation their primary object of concern.

6.0 Sanctifying Grace and the Perpetrator of Abuse

In Catholic thought, 'grace' is a term of art with several layers of meaning. To appreciate the implications of making grace central to the practice of restorative justice one needs to attend to those layers. Orthodox restorative justice theory, with its loose talk of 'grace', 'forgiveness' and 'spirituality', has the effect of uncritically ratifying Catholic calls for restorative justice without attending to these complexities, or even to the particular Catholic approach to crime. As we argue in this section, the logic of the Catholic doctrine of grace would require, in most cases, the pre-eminence of the aim of restoring the offender to the grace of God — a result which sits uncomfortably with orthodox theory's emphasis on the need that restorative programs remain victim-centred.

The Catholic doctrine of grace sets apart Catholicism from various forms of Protestantism. Rooted in St Paul's first century CE writings, it was fully articulated over time, primarily in the writings of St Augustine (354–430) and in the context of the Council of Trent (1545–63), in response to heretic and reformist claims about original sin and free will.

In Catholic thought, grace is a particular kind of spiritual gift freely bestowed by God on human beings, which can be divided into *sanctifying* (or habitual) grace and *actual* grace. Sanctifying grace is the 'supreme grace'.[58] Only those who die in a state of sanctifying grace have a claim to heaven after death. Sanctifying grace changes the nature of those who enjoy it, regenerating them into new life[59] and making them 'partakers of the Divine nature',[60] God's friends[61] and God's sons.[62] The act of establishing this communion with God is called 'justification' and those who are thus 'justified' by grace are called 'the just'.[63] The 'life of grace' that the just enjoy shades into the 'life of glory' characteristic of their afterlife.[64]

Adam and Eve, prior to revolting against God's law, were in a state of 'original justice':[65] they enjoyed, that is, not only sanctifying grace but also 'integrity' — namely 'the perfect subjection of the appetites to reason and of the body to the

---

[58] Joyce George Hayward *The Catholic Doctrine of Grace* Burns Oates and Washbourne London 1920 p 22.

[59] As above at 12; Pohle Joseph and Preuss Arthur *Grace, Actual and Habitual: A Dogmatic Treatise* Herder St Louis 1915 p 272, 312–13, 334.

[60] Joyce above note 58 at 22, see also 35–9; and Pohle and Preuss as above at 340.

[61] Pohle and Preuss as above at 351–5.

[62] Joyce above note 58 at 2–3. See also Pohle and Preuss as above at 356–62.

[63] Joyce as above at 43–5.

[64] As above at 34.

[65] As above at 54–5.

soul'.[66] Upon sinning, they lost both sanctifying grace and integrity, for themselves as well as their offspring.[67] God saw it fit to make the gift of integrity irrecoverable.[68] On the other hand, sanctifying grace can be restored through baptism, which cleanses humans of original sin.[69]

Just as sanctifying grace displaces original sin at the moment of baptism, deliberately committing mortal sin expels sanctifying grace from the sinner[70] (serious sin is called 'mortal' precisely because it extinguishes the life of grace in the soul). Complete sinlessness is unavoidable[71] except by God's special privilege;[72] and venial sin (that is, sin that is either not serious or not fully deliberate)[73] is compatible with the state of grace and does not even diminish it.[74] Mortal sin and grace, however, are radically incompatible. Mortal sin substitutes enmity with God for the Divine sonship and fellowship enjoyed by the just.[75]

The infusion of sanctifying grace into the soul through baptism also confers on the baptised the 'theological virtues': faith in God, the hope or desire to attain or possess Him and charity or love of God.[76] These virtues are called 'theological' because they have God as their direct object.[77] Baptism also bestows, according to most theologians, the so-called 'infused virtues': prudence, justice, fortitude, temperance and others.[78]

In committing mortal sin, the sinner deliberately rejects the love of God. Thus, mortal sin involves the loss of charity as well as sanctifying grace. Faith and hope, however, remain with sinners[79] (only by committing the specific sin of unbelief or infidelity can faith be lost),[80] enabling them to return to God if they are so disposed.[81] In particular, sinners are restored to both grace and charity if they go through the sacrament of penance (confession), feeling 'genuine sorrow', intending to make amends and casting 'out of [their] soul whatever is incompatible with the love of God'.[82]

---

66 As above at 53.

67 As above at 52; Augustin Aurelius 'A Treatise on the Grace of Christ, and on Original Sin' in Philip Schaff (ed.) *A Select Library of the Nicene and Post-Nicene Fathers of the Christian Church, Vol 5 (St Augustin's Anti-Pelagian Writings)* The Christian Literature Company New York 1887 p 217 at 249.

68 Joyce above note 58 at 56; Augustin Aurelius 'A Treatise on Nature and Grace' in Philip Schaff (ed.) *A Select Library of the Nicene and Post-Nicene Fathers of the Christian Church, Vol 5 (St Augustin's Anti-Pelagian Writings)* The Christian Literature Company New York 1887 p 115 at 150.

69 Pohle and Preuss above note 59 at 302–3, 306.

70 As above at 392.

71 Joyce above note 58 at 155.

72 Pohle and Preuss above note 59 at 114.

73 As above at 115.

74 As above at 388

75 Joyce above note 58 at 39–42, 202–3.

76 As above at 76; Pohle and Preuss above note 59 at 339, 363.

77 Joyce as above at 88–9.

78 As above at 89–90; Pohle and Preuss above note 59 at 363.

79 Pohle and Preuss as above at 174, 390; Joyce as above at 203–4.

80 Pohle and Preuss as above at 395–6.

81 Joyce above note 58 at 206.

82 As above at 88.

Sins of the sexual variety feature prominently among those that expel sanctifying grace from the soul, preventing humans from attaining celestial beatitude after death.[83] Child sexual abuse is no exception: in his 'Letter to the Catholics of Ireland' of 2000, Pope Benedict XVI, in urging offending priests to repent and atone for their actions, reminded them that 'Christ's redeeming sacrifice has the power to forgive even the *gravest of sins*, and to bring forth good from even *the most terrible evil.*'[84] This terminology demonstrates that the spiritual condition of the perpetrator of sexual abuse — and in particular the imperative of restoring his justification — has a special urgency from the perspective of the Church. Any Church-run restorative justice processes emphasising *grace*, we argue, must primarily be concerned with the rehabilitation of the offender in the eyes of God: they are 'restorative' primarily in the sense of restoring the offender to the state of sanctifying grace.

In centring *grace*, Catholic justice entails that concern for the survivor will in many (but not all) cases be of secondary importance. Unlike offenders, victims have not, by virtue of the sin of abuse, lost justification. To be sure, we cannot be certain of whether or not they are justified; this, however, is simply the uncertainty that attends everyone's justification, for we can never be altogether sure to have met all the prerequisites for receiving sanctifying grace.[85] The victims' salvation is as important as everyone's, but the Church has no reason to believe that it is in jeopardy more than anyone else's. In the case of the abuser, on the contrary, it has compelling reasons for believing just that: assuming the perpetrator had been justified prior to the abuse, he necessarily lost justification upon committing abuse — a mortal sin. Spiritually speaking, then, the offender needs more assistance than the victim.

This does not mean that, when Catholic advocates of restorative justice cite restoring faith to the survivor as the primary goal of the process, they are being dishonest. *In those cases where victims have lost faith as a result of the abuse*, the logic of grace does require that the Church's concern for survivors be of overriding importance. This is because theological faith is '"the beginning, the foundation, and the root of all justification"'.[86] While perpetrators have lost justification upon committing the abuse, they have not thereby foregone the foundation of justification (faith), as this is only lost through the specific sin of unbelief. Victims who have lapsed into unbelief, on the other hand, have lost that very foundation: thus, their prospects of salvation are in even greater jeopardy than those of their abusers. Concern for such victims — the logic of grace demands — will necessarily be the foremost priority. It is important to stress, however, that it is only in the subset of sexual abuse cases involving victims who have lost faith that the logic of grace would require restorative justice to be victim-centred in this way. Furthermore, considering the sinful nature of unbelief, there is a real risk that an unbelieving survivor would psychologically experience as a form of victim-blaming any Church-run processes aimed at assisting their conversion.

---

[83] Pohle and Preuss above note 59 at 394.

[84] Pope Benedict XVI in Robertson Geoffrey *The Case of the Pope* Penguin London 2010 p 38–9 (emphasis added).

[85] Pohle and Preuss above note 59 at 380.

[86] Cited in Pohle and Preuss above note 59 at 182.

7.0 Actual Grace and the Perpetrator of Abuse

The idea of sanctifying grace does not exhaust the Catholic doctrine of grace. If the concept of sanctifying grace explains why Catholic restorative justice needs to take the spiritual wellbeing of perpetrators as an especially serious concern, the concept of actual grace helps us understand how both perpetrators and survivors are positioned vis-à-vis that concern, as well as the demands made of them.

Actual graces are spiritual gifts from God — temporary 'motions' non-deterministically[87] 'impelling the soul to this or that act'[88] by way of illuminating the mind and strengthening of the will.[89] They are experienced as 'transient impulses' of the soul[90] and are necessary in order to enable humans 'to perform salutary acts'.[91] '[S]alutary acts are those directed to the attainment of sanctifying grace'.[92] Thus, actual graces are gifts conducive and necessary to the acquisition, maintenance and restoration of sanctifying grace.[93] For example, in order for mentally competent adults to receive baptism, they need to possess certain internal states (faith in God, sorrow for past sins, and so on) that make them suitable recipients of sanctifying grace.[94] These internal states are themselves supernatural gifts of God — instances of 'actual grace' preparing their souls for the further gift of sanctifying grace.[95]

Maintaining sanctifying grace ('perseverance in grace')[96] by avoiding mortal sin on anything more than a temporary basis similarly requires the assistance of actual grace.[97] The main reason why humans need these actual graces 'over and above the … endowment of [theological and infused] virtues'[98] granted together with sanctifying grace is that, as we have seen, baptism does not also restore 'integrity'. As a result, humans in the state of justification remain besieged by temptations and ready to yield to 'concupiscence'.[99] Actual grace temporarily heals this 'weakness of the will' resulting from original sin,[100] enabling humans to fend off temptations to commit mortal sin.[101] Thus, the actual grace consisting in the fear of offending God may aid the infused virtue of temperance to keep the just from giving in to sensualism.[102]

---

[87] As above at 32; Joyce above note 58 at 129.
[88] Joyce as above at 146.
[89] Pohle and Preuss above note 59 at 19–26; see also Augustin above note 67 at 218–23, 226.
[90] Pohle and Preuss as above at 12.
[91] As above at 1, 110.
[92] As above at 82.
[93] As above at 14–15, 271.
[94] Joyce above note 58 at 120–3.
[95] As above at 125–8.
[96] As above at 142.
[97] Pohle and Preuss above note 59 at 123–4.
[98] Joyce above note 58 at 146.
[99] As above at 144–5; Pohle and Preuss above note 59 at 113–14. Augustin quotes John to describe 'cupidity' as 'that "lust of the flesh, and the lust of the eyes, and the pride of life, which is not of the Father, but is of the world"'. Augustin above note 67 at 224.
[100] Pohle and Preuss above note 59 at 16.
[101] As above at 65.
[102] Joyce above note 59 at 147–9.

When humans lose justification as a result of committing mortal sin they can regain it by repenting.[103] Repentance is itself a gift from God — that is, an actual grace — as sinners 'deprived of sanctifying grace cannot by [their] natural powers take a single step towards' justification.[104] If actual grace has the effect of infallibly moving the recipient to do the act for which the grace was granted (for example the act of repentance), the grace is called 'efficacious', otherwise it is merely a 'sufficient' grace.[105] Because God's mercy is universal, he wants everyone's salvation:[106] this means that He grants *sufficient* actual graces to all, even great sinners.[107] This includes, of course, the perpetrators of sexual abuse. But a *sufficient* actual grace will not infallibly move the recipient to do the salutary act of repentance which will enable him to re-enter into the fold of sanctifying grace. The actual grace needs to be *efficacious*.

As the efficacy of actual grace is a function of the response made to it by the recipient's will,[108] the Church will be anxious, in clerical sexual abuse cases, to create the conditions conducive to the perpetrator's will appropriately responding to actual grace. The doctrine of justification insists that no-one can know 'with certainty of faith whether [they are] justified or not'.[109] If it is always open to question whether *anyone* is in the state of sanctifying grace, the concern will logically be heightened in respect of anyone who is known to have committed mortal sin — particularly if, as in the case of perpetrators of sexual abuse, they have been repeat offenders over the course of many years. While it cannot be ruled out that, after the acts of abuse, a perpetrator has already positively responded to the actual graces afforded him by God, feeling genuine repentance, performing penance and thus recovering sanctifying grace, the Church can hardly be expected to be complacent and leave the offender to his own devices. Thus, the logic of grace suggests that Catholic restorative justice would aim to bring about the conditions under which the actual graces afforded by God to the offender with a view to his repentance may become efficacious, leading to the offender's recovery of sanctifying grace.

The Church's assistance, by way of restorative justice programs, in bringing about these conditions will be particularly necessary when, as in many of the clerical abuse cases, the sin was habitual. In these cases, it is more than possible that the sinner is of the obdurate (impenitent)[110] variety — the kind whose heart has been 'darkened', whom God has given 'up to uncleanness', leading him to sin even more, doing 'things [that are] so sins themselves, that they [are] also the penalties of [initial]

---

[103] As above at 208–9.
[104] As above at 205.
[105] As above at 138–9; Pohle and Preuss above note 59 at 41. The way in which human free will and divine grace interact to produce salutary acts is the object of theological difficulties. Pohle and Preuss as above at 40, 222–69; Joyce as above at 66. Catholic thought struggles to reconcile its commitment to the idea of free will with the idea that humans are naturally incapable of performing salutary acts without God's assistance (as salutary acts are oriented to a supernatural aim). Pohle and Preuss as above at 18, 82–100 and Joyce as above at 56–7. See also Augustin above note 67 at 226–7.
[106] Pohle and Preuss as above at 156–7.
[107] As above at 167; Joyce above note 58 at 130.
[108] Pohle and Preuss as above at 43.
[109] As above at 379.
[110] Pohle and Preuss above note 59 at 172–3.

sins'.[111] Obdurate sinners are not granted actual grace in the form of repentance itself, but only lesser actual graces.[112] These lesser spiritual gifts *may* eventually lead them to repent and reattain justification, but this may prove a formidable task for them without the dedicated support of the Church.

In sum, the doctrine of grace suggests that Catholic restorative justice in cases of clerical sexual abuse should be directed at facilitating the process through which offenders can cooperate with the *sufficient* actual graces granted to obdurate sinners. Additionally or alternatively, the doctrine of grace makes it imperative for Catholic restorative justice to facilitate the perpetrators' performance of acts that will merit for them *efficacious* actual graces infallibly leading to their recovery of sanctifying grace. This is because, according to most theologians, sinners can obtain 'the dispositions necessary for justification' in the form of actual graces merited 'by good works'[113] — namely, morally good actions that are freely performed and ultimately done in the service of God (out of love for Him, or at least out of a desire to obey His commands, and so on).[114]

8.0 Actual Grace and the Survivor of Abuse

We have argued that the logic of the discourse of grace entails the risk that survivors of clerical child sexual abuse will not be the principal object of moral concern in Catholic restorative justice programs emphasising grace (unless their spiritual state requires urgent attention by reason of their having lapsed into unbelief). Furthermore, the doctrine of grace suggests that survivors may be involved in the rather demanding capacity of rehabilitators of their abusers, through the practice of forgiveness. This follows from what the doctrine of grace has to say about 'good works'. Through good works, the just may merit final perseverance as well as an increase in their sanctifying grace.[115] The increase in grace is proportional to the will's commitment to the act, to the intensity of the charity that animates it and to the difficulty of the act itself: forgiving a grave wrong deserves a greater reward than forgiving a light one.[116] Significantly, however, the good works performed by the just may also merit an increase in grace, final perseverance and conversion from mortal sin *for others*.[117] Forgiving abuse (a mortal sin) qualifies precisely as the kind of highly meritorious good work by which the victim of abuse might deserve a considerable increase in sanctifying

[111] Augustin above note 67 at 129.
[112] Joyce above note 58 at 205–7.
[113] Pohle and Preuss above note 59 at 431.
[114] As above at 397, 410–17; Joyce above note 58 at 164–5, 173–4.
[115] Pohle and Preuss as above at 384–5, 401, 432–4.
[116] Joyce above note 58 at 176–7. Grace is by definition an undeserved gift. Paul 'Titus' in United States Conference of Catholic Bishops *The New American Bible, Revised Edition* (NABRE) USCCB Publishing 2011 § 3.5 available online at: <http://www.usccb.org/bible/titus/3>accessed on…; Pohle and Preuss above note 59 at 131; Augustin above note 67 at 122–3. Grace is not a requirement of justice, but issues from 'pure benevolence' and 'sheer love'. Pohle and Preuss above note 69 at 6, 7; see also Augustin above note 67 at 225. Thus, it is the good work itself, rather than the human performing it, that merits an increase in grace as its reward. Pohle and Preuss above note 59 at 38, 138; Augustin above note 67 at 234; Joyce above note 58 at 161–4.
[117] Pohle and Preuss as above at 432, 433–4.

grace for him/herself and, more importantly, actual graces for the abuser — thereby facilitating his restoration to justification.

Forgiveness, however, is a highly contentious demand to make of victims, especially survivors of child sexual abuse. Forgiveness forms an important point of contention in feminist critiques of restorative justice. Although 'resolutely embedded in restorative justice *processes*', forgiveness has largely remained 'out of sight of examination' in mainstream and Christian restorative justice scholarship.[118] When it is discussed, theorists remain divided about what forgiveness entails beyond 'a change in motivation toward the offender'.[119] Hence Armour and Umbreit caution that, in general, restorative justice proponents must clarify the role of forgiveness and provide guidance to practitioners to prevent a 'reductionism' that might distort the healing potential of any processes, especially among religious victims 'who have been told by their clergy that they must forgive in accordance with the tenets of their religion'.[120] Victim respondents to the Irish Study 'had a lot to say' about forgiveness and apology. Some viewed apology as a primary function of the process of individual accountability by the offender, while others 'were concerned that the offender might be seeking to manipulate the victim into forgiving them for selfish rather than genuine reasons'.[121]

It cannot be ruled out that survivors may experience a call for forgiveness in empowering ways, particularly as it has an intriguing potential for reversing — within the domain of spiritual relations — the power dynamic between victim and abuser, as hoped by Hudson and others.[122] Indeed, the more obdurate the sinner, the more he will be likely to *need*, according to the logic of grace, the victim's good works on his behalf. At the same time, any call for forgiveness may all too easily turn into a psychologically burdensome responsibility — an emotionally exploitative imperative, even — to forgive. This seems particularly likely, given the implication following from the discourse of grace that any internal appeal to forgive presenting itself to the victim's mind must be an actual grace coming from God and demanding the cooperation of the survivor's will.

The concerns voiced by Stubbs about the use or abuse of emotion in restorative practices are highly pertinent in this context, and appear to mirror the more strident arguments made *for* restorative justice in the context of spirituality and faith.[123] Some Catholic restorative justice mediators do indeed describe their work in terms of invoking emotions from Church representatives and complainants. The power of the mediation is associated with the 'emotional connection and energy that flows from the interaction between the giver and the receiver. It is the sharing of this emotional experience that gives the apology its healing force'.[124] To avoid the 'reductionism'

118 Armour and Umbreit above note 27 at 126. Emphasis added.
119 As above at 125.
120 As above at 125–6.
121 Keenan above note 5 at 178.
122 See above note 9.
123 See above note 26.
124 Rooney Greg (VIC) *The Royal Commission into Institutional Responses to Child Sexual Abuse* Submission with Respect Towards Healing, the Melbourne Response and Meeting the Needs of the Victims of Sexual Abuse (2013). p 111 <http://www.childabuseroyalcommission.gov.au/getattachment/

forewarned by Armour and Umbreit, Church-appointed mediators must be aware of their own emotional desires for outcomes, and that they are 'not an empty vessel';[125] instead, they bring with them personal spiritual and ideological 'prejudices, beliefs and emotional reactions',[126] particularly those favouring grace as salvation for the offender as the foremost priority of mediation.

9.0 Conclusions

Appeals to the healing potential of 'grace' and 'forgiveness' are central to much restorative justice scholarship. This literature, however, does not adequately explain the meaning or use of 'grace' which, we have argued, has a range of precise and technical meanings within Catholic thought. It is only by clarifying and interrogating these meanings that a fuller understanding can be gained of what is envisioned by Catholic restorative justice, especially in the context of clerical child sexual abuse where the Church has internationally moved into the terrain of alternative dispute resolution through the implementation of in-house mediation schemes. In restorative justice scholarship, 'forgiveness' occupies in general a confused or contested position, the emotionally exploitative risks of which feminist criminologists have highlighted in the context of gender-based offences such as sexual abuse.

The trite use of complex concepts such as 'grace' by advocates of restorative justice lends itself to manipulation in ways that are detrimental to victims of sexual crime. These problems are compounded, we have argued, by the fact that the unreflective use of these concepts in orthodox scholarship has the effect of ratifying and lending authority to religious understandings of 'grace' that are odds with the purportedly victim-centred ethos of restorative justice. The Catholic doctrine of grace entails that in the context of Catholic restorative justice the goal of restoring justice to victims who have not lapsed into unbelief would take second place to the goal of restoring justification to the offender. Hence Catholic advocacy of restorative justice in cases of clerical child sexual abuse warrants especially careful scrutiny in light of well-established feminist critiques of restorative justice in the context of sexual crime.

---

afd9b78b-4283-4699-a391-60e026205211/19-Greg-Rooney> Accessed 30 August 2015. Rooney Greg and Ross Margaret 'Mediating Between Victims of Sexual Abuse and Religious Institutions' (2007) 18 *Australasian Dispute Resolution Journal* 10 at 15.

[125] Rooney *Submission* as above at 113.

[126] Rooney and Ross above note 124 at 13.

Sin, Silence and States of Denial: Canon Law and the 'Discovery' of Child Sexual Abuse

Timothy Willem Jones

Abstract. In discussions of the sexual assault of minors, feminists, historians of sexuality and religious authorities are in uncommon agreement. They concur that, although minors have been subject to sexual assault throughout the modern era, the late 1970s and 1980s saw a new 'discovery' of the phenomenon. This discovery initially was located in feminist critiques of male violence within the family, but quickly spread to other sites: homosexuals, paedophile rings, satanic ritual abuse and most recently clerical sexual abuse. Recent inquiries into sexual abuse in Christian Churches have collated data of abuse on a scale hitherto unimagined. The data suggests that abuse was most prevalent between 1945 and 1980, the period prior to the articulation of feminist critiques of sexual violence. Many have sought to explain this historic 'black spot' as the product of a failure of comprehension. Feminists have claimed that their articulation of sexual politics was required before child sexual victimhood could be recognised. Church authorities, on the other hand, have repeatedly stated that their failure to respond appropriately to allegations of abuse was because such abuse was 'unthinkable'. This paper seeks to complicate these explanations of historic blindness to child sexual abuse by examining the capacity of church law to comprehend and articulate the harms of child sexual abuse prior to the feminist critiques of the 1970s.

1.0 Introduction: The Late 'Discovery' of Clerical Child Sexual Abuse

In discussions of the sexual assault of minors, feminists, historians of sexuality and religious authorities are in uncommon agreement. They concur that, although minors have been subject to sexual assault throughout the modern era, and there had been moments of social awareness in the past, particularly between the 1880s and the 1920s, this recognition of the harms of adult sex with minors was precarious, contested and was effectively silenced until the late 1970s and 1980s saw a new 'discovery' of the phenomenon. This discovery initially was located in feminist critiques of male violence within the family, but quickly spread to other sites: homosexuals, paedophile rings, satanic ritual abuse and, most recently, clerical sexual abuse.

The articulation of this '(re)discovery' differs only a little across these three diverse fields. Historians of sexuality have observed that although Richard Krafft-Ebing coined the term 'paedophilia' around 1886, and there were periodic moments of concern about sex with minors, it did not become a major and abiding social concern until the later twentieth century. Prior to the 1970s, psychiatrists and psychoanalysts saw the problem as rare and relatively trivial. In the mid-twentieth century child sex offenders, along with homosexuals, transsexuals and other sexual 'deviants', were treated with a range of psychological therapies including hormonal and aversion therapies. Their offences were regarded as symptomatic of a constitutional psychic weakness: uncommon personal failings 'to be pitied rather than punished'.[1] Conversely, as Steven Angelides has written, their child victims 'were routinely rendered sexually flirtatious, precocious and even seductive'.[2]

This all changed from the late 1970s. A greater openness in sexual attitudes following the sexual revolution, feminist critiques of patriarchy including domestic violence and sexual assault and a new legal discourse of children's rights created conditions in which sex with minors could be articulated as 'Child Sexual Abuse'.[3] This reformulation — of 'sex-with-minors' as 'CSA' — created the conditions for the issue to dominate media, government agendas and (to a lesser extent) child protection services from the 1980s. Feminist critiques of institutionalised patriarchy, in particular, were central to the recognition of harm in CSA.[4] Asserting the essential 'innocence' and powerlessness of the child victim, 1970s feminists refocused attention on the offender.[5] The 'paedophile' came to be identified as a distinct, abhorrent pathological identity to be treated as an *a priori* criminal. As historian Shurlee Swain has demonstrated, locating CSA in a broader critique of male power 'saw child sexual abuse removed from the realm of individual pathology and acknowledged as a social and political issue demanding action from governments and the courts'.[6]

In their evidence in recent Australian inquiries, church authorities have presented a similar narrative. Universally they lament the past failures of their institutions, but go on to explain it as a failure of interpretation. In the past, they understood child sexual abuse primarily as a sin (to be resolved through forgiveness), and later as pathological behavior (to be resolved through therapy). Only in recent times, they say, was it

[1] Jenkins Philip *Moral Panic: Changing Concepts of the Child Molester in Modern America* Yale University Press New Haven 1998.

[2] Angelides Steven 'The Emergence of the Paedophile in the late Twentieth Century' (2005) 36 (126) *Australian Historical Studies* 278.

[3] Scott Denise and Swain Shurlee *Confronting Cruelty: Historical Perspectives on Child Protection* Melbourne University Press Melbourne 2002.

[4] Olafson Erna, Corwin David and Summit Roland 'Modern History of Child Sexual Abuse Awareness: Cycles of Discovery and Suppression' (1993) 17 (1) *Child Abuse and Neglect* 17.

[5] See, for example, the foundational work of Louise Armstrong, Susan Brownmuller, Sandra Butler and Linda Gordon. Armstrong Louise *Kiss Daddy Goodnight: A Speak Out on Incest* Pocket Books New York 1978; Brownmuller Susan *Against Our Will: Men, Women and Rape* Bantam Books New York 1975; Butler Sandra *Conspiracy of Silence: The Trauma of Incest* Volcano Press San Francisco 1978; Gordon Linda *Heroes of their own Lives: The Politics and History of Family Violence* Viking Penguin New York 1988.

[6] Swain Shurlee 'Giving Voice to Narratives of Institutional Sex Abuse' (2015) 41 (2) *Australian Feminist Law Journal* in this issue. See also Kitzinger Jenny 'Transformations of Public and Private Knowledge: Audience Reception, Feminism and the Experience of Childhood Sexual Abuse' (2001) 1 (1) *Feminist Media Studies* 91.

understood as a crime (requiring a criminal justice response). Evidence in the transcripts of the 2013 Victorian Parliamentary Inquiry into the Handling of Child Sexual Abuse by Religious and Other Organisations amply illustrates this strange myopia. For example, Fr G. Chambers, the provincial of the Salesians of Don Bosco, stated that child sexual abuse 'was probably seen as a sinful offence. I think only as time progressed did it become a crime against the individual, a crime against society, a crime before the nation of Australia'.[7] Similarly, Br T. Graham, provincial of the Hospitaller Order of St John of God admitted that in the past the church saw CSA as a sin, rather than a crime, but that now 'it has shifted beyond that and is clearly indicating that it considers it not only a sinful activity but a criminal activity'.[8] The testimony of the Christian Brothers was even more revealing. Br J. McDonald, the deputy province leader, explained the Order's failure to deal with two known abusers 'because of the whole understanding of paedophilic behaviour'. He stated that 'it was treated as a moral failure, then eventually it came to be understood as a psychosexual dysfunction'.[9] He admitted that although they did not treat it as such, 'every leader of the Christian Brothers should have known' that child sexual abuse is 'a terrible crime that has ruined lives'.[10]

This concurrence between historians of sexuality, feminists and church authorities regarding an historic insensitivity to child sexual assault prior to the 1970s is unsettling. Particularly disturbing is the fact that the decades before the feminist articulation of child sex abuse in the 1970s and 1980s — this time of denial — correspond with what appears to be the historic period in which CSA in religious institutions was at its worst. In data from *Towards Healing*, the main procedure for responding to victims' claims in the Australian Catholic Church after 1996, 76 per cent of complaints related to allegations of CSA in the period 1950 to 1980.[11] A similar pattern was also found in the highly regarded John Jay College study of abuse in the US Catholic Church.[12] At the time when abuse was most rampant, it was apparently also least visible. The invisibility of abuse, or at least the seemingly endemic denial of its harms and criminality, is remarkable, especially in institutions like those appearing before the Victorian Parliamentary Inquiry cited above. These institutions were subject to some of the highest numbers of allegations of abuse. In the Hospitaller Order of St John of God, for example, over 70 per cent of brothers were subject to credible allegations of abuse.[13] In circumstances such as these, how

---

[7] Parliament of Victoria, Family and Community Development Committee *Inquiry into the Handling of Child Abuse by Religious and Other Organisations* (2013) Salesians of Don Bosco Transcript 29 April p 3.

[8] Parliament of Victoria, Family and Community Development Committee *Inquiry into the Handling of Child Abuse by Religious and Other Organisations* (2013) St John of God Oceania Province Transcript 29 April p 20.

[9] Parliament of Victoria, Family and Community Development Committee *Inquiry into the Handling of Child Abuse by Religious and Other Organisations* (2013) Christian Brothers Transcript 3 May p 4.

[10] As above.

[11] Royal Commission into Institutional Responses to Child Sexual Abuse Transcript of Public Hearing (day 24) 9 December 2013 p 2477.

[12] John Jay College of Criminal Justice *The Nature and Scope of Sexual Abuse of Minors by Catholic Priests and Deacons in the United States, 1950–2002* Supplementary Report (2006) p 7.

[13] Callinan Rory and Tove Josephine 'Pell Urged to Close Order Over Abuses' *Sydney Morning Herald* 12 November 2012 <http://www.smh.com.au/national/pell-urged-to-close-order-over-abuses-20121111-296h2.html> Accessed 26 August 2015.

could anyone 'turn a blind eye' to the assault of children? Or see it as sinful action but not as a crime? Were there really not the conditions of possibility for a fuller recognition of the harms of abuse prior to the 1970s?

2.0 Moral Panics and Cultures of Denial

The processes by which attention came to be focused on the apparently new social phenomenon of child sexual abuse at particular moments in history have been well researched. Stanley Cohen and Philip Jenkins' work on 'moral panics' has been particularly influential.[14] Their explication of the reasons why paedophilia captured the public imagination at particular moments in time is persuasive and their critique of media focus on the worst, atypical offenders has political utility. As Marie Keenan observes, the strategies developed by Cohen and others open the 'complexities of the issues involved in power, knowledge, sexuality, childhood, adulthood, desire and the fate of the body', obscured by moral panics, to scholarly investigation.[15] However, the wider political project out of which the concept of moral panics was developed — the relativisation of deviance — poses problems for research into child sex offenders.

There is a danger that framing CSA as a 'moral panic' and figuring the child sex offender as a 'folk devil' could work to obscure the gravity of the offences being studied. This difficulty is evident in Jenkins' work from the 1990s, which could be read to explain the emergence of panic about 'paedophile priests' in the US Catholic Church as an exaggerated response to sectarian conflict.[16] Jenkins does not disregard the severity of child sex offences, but by critiquing the social and cultural factors that gave the CSA crisis in the US Catholic Church its force, he inevitably downplays its significance. As Jenkins later observed, 'whoever heard of a *legitimate* panic, or of a *well founded* hysteria?'.[17] Chris Greer and Eugene McLaughlin have advanced a similar, but more politically neutral, model to describe the processes by which institutions and society come to attend to specific phenomena, such as CSA. Focusing on the transition between 'latent' and 'activated' scandals, they avoid the emotional weight of the word 'panic'.[18] Like Cohen's 'moral panics', their study of the dynamics of institutional CSA scandals illuminates the ways in which controversies come to public view. Yet it does not explain why people did not attend to abuse at other times; neither does Jenkins' useful explication of factors that might lead to a particular scandal's 'failure to launch'.[19]

---

[14] Jenkins above note 1 and Cohen Stanley *Folk Devils and Moral Panics: The Creation of the Mods and Rockers* Routledge Oxford 2011 (1972).

[15] Keenan Marie *Child Sexual Abuse and the Catholic Church* Oxford University Press Oxford 2012 p 100.

[16] Jenkins Philip *Pedophiles and Priests: Anatomy of a Contemporary Crisis* Oxford University Press New York 1996.

[17] Jenkins Philip 'Failure to Launch: Why Do Some Social Issues Fail to Detonate Moral Panics' (2009) 49 *British Journal of Criminology* 35.

[18] Greer Chris and McLaughlin Eugene 'The Sir Jimmy Savile Scandal: Child Sexual Abuse and Institutional Denial at the BBC' (2013) 9 (3) *Crime Media Culture* 243.

[19] Jenkins above note 17 at 45.

Why individuals, institutions and societies panic about serious social and moral problems is a different question to why they ignore them. By focusing on how CSA came to be recognised as a serious problem, narratives about the late 'discovery' of child abuse produced by feminists, historians of sexuality and church authorities have also neglected this question. For as is apparent in the testimony of religious authorities and medical experts, the sexual assault of children was known about prior to the formulation of 'CSA' as a major social problem. Yet this knowledge was able to be contained, ignored and denied in such a way that its criminal nature was elided. In what follows I examine the techniques through which the criminality of child sexual assault was silenced. For, as an examination of canon law reveals, the silencing of abuse in the middle of the twentieth century was an active process, a process of keeping knowledge at bay. Particular techniques were deployed to resist the recognition of harm and maintain a state of denial.

Towards the end of his life, Stanley Cohen inverted his work on 'moral panics' to explore the question of how we keep disturbing knowledge at bay.[20] Outlining a preliminary 'sociology of denial', Cohen described different types, agents and ways of not knowing. Literal denial is the simplest type: the assertion that something is untrue. Interpretive denial, on the other hand, is not the denial of facts, but ascribing to them different meanings. Implicatory denial refuses neither facts, nor conventional interpretations, but rather 'the psychological, political or moral implications that conventionally follow'.[21] Denial may be individual, official or cultural. It may be historical or contemporary. Things may be denied by victims, perpetrators or bystanders. These different states of denial interact and inform each other. They may not always be problematic, as those psychic defence mechanisms which use denial to keep personal trauma at bay illustrate. But, as in the case of church authorities refusing to know enough about clerical sex offenders, they may also facilitate the perpetration of atrocities.

In Cohen's account, the opposite of denial is acknowledgement. Feminist consciousness-raising is a paradigmatic mode of combating denial, and acknowledging discomforting situations. In the growth of awareness of CSA that followed feminist actions from the late 1970s, particular attention was paid to the silencing potential of psychoanalysis. As feminist criminologist Carol Smart has argued, this has continued to the point of overemphasis

> and insufficient attention [has been] paid to the role of the legal establishment and the practices of the criminal justice system in the persistent, but multifaceted, inability to define adult/child sexual contact as abusive or harmful.[22]

This neglect of the role of law in the denial of CSA is also evident in church law.

---

[20] Cohen Stanley *States of Denial: Knowing about Atrocities and Suffering* Polity Press Cambridge 2001.

[21] As above at 8.

[22] Smart Carol 'Reconsidering the Recent History of Child Sexual Abuse, 1910–1960' (2000) 29 (1) *Journal of Social Policy* 55. See also Smart Carol 'A History of Ambivalence and Conflict in the Discursive Construction of the "Child Victim" of Sexual Abuse' (1999) 8 *Social & Legal Studies* 391.

Although non-familial child sex crimes were legislated against and policed with particular fervour in the period following second-wave feminism, the earlier period — of denial — was not without legal tools for the discipline of clerical sex offenders. In fact, the major Christian churches were aware of abuse in this period and had long-standing practices for the treatment of clerical sexual offenders. However, as my case studies will show, these practices have been less visible because they were often not specifically addressed to 'Child Sexual Abuse'. In order to uncover the treatment of clerical child sex offenders prior to the reframing of CSA in the 1970s and 1980s, a broader category of sexual offence needs to be examined that attends to changes in legal and medical history. Drawing on Cohen's late work on the sociology of denial, I will examine two historical case studies to explore how attention to the law, in relation to theology and medicine, might complicate narratives of a late discovery of clerical child sexual abuse. These are: first, the articulation of child sex crimes in the canon law of the Roman Catholic Church across the twentieth century; and second, the extra-canonical legal processes developed in the Church of England for the governance and discipline of clerical sex offenders from 1870 to the 1960s.

3.0 Case Study One: Roman Catholic Canon Law, 1917–2001

Child sexual abuse by clergy has been a crime in Roman Catholic ecclesiastical law from the earliest records of church governance and this has been restated periodically throughout the history of the church.[23] In both the 1917 and 1983 Codes of Canon Law it is clearly characterised as a crime for which a priest can be punished, including by being deposed from the clerical state, or laicised. Two areas of canon law are particularly important in relation to the discipline of clergy for child sex abuse. The first is the section describing violations of clerical chastity.[24] In both the 1917 and 1983 codes, sex with a minor under the age of sixteen is listed with other crimes against the sixth commandment (prohibiting adultery) such as attempted marriage, concubinage, rape and other sexual offences.[25] Clerics guilty of these crimes are 'to be punished with just penalties, not excluding dismissal from the clerical state if the case so warrants'.[26] The second is the section on the solicitation of sex during the sacrament of confession.[27] A priest who solicits a penitent to sexual sin in, or in association with, confession 'is to be punished, according to the gravity of the delict, by suspension, prohibitions, and

[23] Anderson Colt 'When Magisterium Becomes Imperium: Peter Damian on the Accountability of Bishops for Scandal' (2004) 65 (4) *Theological Studies* 741; Daly Brendan 'Priestly Celibacy: The Obligations of Continence and Celibacy for Priests' (2009) 4 *Compass* 20.

[24] *Code of Canon Law* (1983) [hereafter CIC83] can 277 details the requirements of clerical chastity, and empowers bishops to pass judgment concerning its observance. The authoritative text of CIC83 is in Latin. An English translation of CIC83 prepared under the auspices of the Canon Law Society of America is available online: http://www.vatican.va/archive/ENG1104/_INDEX.HTM.

[25] *Code of Canon Law* (1917) [hereafter CIC17] cann 2358–9; CIC83 cann 1394–5. The *Code of Canons of the Eastern Churches* (1990) [CCEO] does not explicitly mention sex with minors in its equivalent section, but they would be included in 'sins against chastity'. CCEO can 1453.

[26] CIC83 can 1395 §2. The 1917 code states that they 'are suspended, declared infamous, and are deprived of any office, benefice, dignity, responsibility, if they have such, whatsoever, and in more serious cases they are to be deposed' (CIC17 can 2359 §2).

[27] CIC17 cann 904 and 2368; CIC83 can 1387.

privations; in graver cases he is to be dismissed from the clerical state'.[28] This inherently includes penitents who are minors.

The canon law of the Roman Catholic Church was uniformly codified for the first time in 1917. The universal law is adjudicated in local ecclesiastical courts and follows a continental inquisitorial style of proceeding. The basic jurisdictional units in Roman Catholic governance are dioceses and religious institutes. Dioceses are usually geographical units governed by a bishop. Religious institutes, commonly called religious orders, are governed by a major superior who is the head of the institute. They are comprised of their membership, which may be spread around the world. Each diocese or group of dioceses would normally have an ecclesiastical court or tribunal. In modern times, these are almost exclusively occupied with marriage annulments. If a criminal penal trail of a priest were to be held, a college of at least three judges, or judicial vicars, would be required to try the case.[29] Canon law demands a particularly high standard of proof for a determination of guilt, known as 'moral certainty'. This is a similar standard to 'beyond reasonable doubt' in criminal law, and manifestly higher than the standards of probability used in civil law. Normally at least two witnesses or indisputable documentary evidence is required before a canonical penalty can be imposed.[30]

While canon law functions to order and discipline the Catholic Church, its underlying principles differ significantly from secular legal systems. The church has a fundamental metaphysical purpose: the eternal salvation of its members. As CIC83, can 1752 states, 'the salvation of souls ... must always be the supreme law in the Church'. In secular criminal law, if a person is found guilty of a crime, justice would demand that an appropriate punishment is given. In canon law, however, punishment is a last resort. The primary purpose of sanctions in the penal canons is remedial, to 'encourage the offender's change of mind and heart'.[31] Only a few canons provide for 'expiatory' or 'vindictive' penalties, which do not depend on the reformation of the offender but are retributive. As a general norm, CIC 83, can 1341 states that:

> An ordinary is to take care to initiate a judicial or administrative process to impose or declare penalties only after he has ascertained that fraternal correction or rebuke or other means of pastoral solicitude cannot sufficiently repair the scandal, restore justice, reform the offender.

[28] CIC83 can 1387. The 1917 code is more explicit: CIC17 can 2368 states that: 'Anyone who has committed the crime of solicitation ... is to be suspended from celebrating Mass and hearing sacramental confessions and, if the gravity of the crime calls for it, he is to be declared unfit for hearing them; he is to be deprived of all benefices and ranks, of the right to vote or be voted for, and is to be declared unfit for all of them, and in more serious cases he is to be reduced to the lay state'. Furthermore, the 1917 code requires penitents who have been solicited to report it to the bishop or the Holy Office within a month of the event (CIC17 can 904). This requirement was not maintained in CIC83.

[29] The full procedure for canonical trials is detailed in book VII of CIC83 cann 1400–1752.

[30] CIC83 can 1573.

[31] Coughlin John *Canon Law: A Comparative Study with Anglo-America Legal Theory* Oxford University Press Oxford 2011 p 85. See also Coriden James *An Introduction to Canon Law* Paulist Press New York 2004 p 5–6.

Before proceeding with a criminal penal trial, according to canon law a bishop must first determine if resolution can be achieved through pastoral means. Mindful of the preference of CIC83 can 1342 for judicial proceedings in the imposition of penalties, he may also proceed through executive administrative action rather than a formal trial.[32] It is, as John Paul II stated in his introduction to CIC83, 'justice based on charity'.

The two principles outlined above — that the law is to be pastoral and that bishops have the authority to dispense from the general laws of the church — are attractive in many contexts. However, they also have the potential to contravene a principle of natural justice: that no-one should be a judge in their own cause (*nemo iudex in causa sua*). As Gillian Evans observed:

> within an episcopal church the bishop has inalienably embedded in his office both a pastoral and a judicial relationship to his priests, so that the breach of the *nemo iudex* principle is, at it were, almost built in.[33]

Even if in modern times it has been rare, perhaps unknown, for a bishop to directly adjudicate in an ecclesiastical tribunal, prior to 2001 it was solely the bishop's decision whether to initiate a criminal penal trial or respond with fraternal correction or pastoral solicitude. This conflict of interest has proved to be gravely problematic in dealing with the discipline of clergy for the sexual abuse of children.

In Australia, for example, up until 30 September 2013 *Towards Healing*, the Church's principal procedure to respond to people who have been sexually abused by a priest, religious or other Catholic Church personnel, had received at least 2215 complaints of abuse.[34] Yet, it appears that no Australian bishop has ever initiated a trial in a canonical court for sexual offences against a minor.[35] There is no official public record of what other disciplinary processes have been applied to sexually offending clergy in Australia, although there are now data from the UN Committee Against Torture on the Vatican's sentences for clergy globally since 2001.

The significance of Australian bishops' decisions not to proceed judicially is unambiguous. The 1983 code is clear in its preference for 'judicial rather than administrative procedure in the imposition of penalties to protect better the rights of all concerned (c.1342)'. And further, 'the code explicitly requires judicial process for perpetual, or irrevocable, penalties such as deprivation of office (c.1336, §1, 3°)'.[36] Assuming they were proceeding canonically, by choosing to proceed extra-judicially, ordinaries

[32] CIC83 cann 1717–19; CIC17 cann 1939–46.

[33] Evans Gillian *Discipline and Justice in the Church of England* Gracewing Leominster 1998 p 78.

[34] Royal Commission above note 11. These data are incomplete for *Towards Healing*, and do not include allegations dealt with through the *Melbourne Response* or through secular avenues of redress.

[35] Information on penal trails was requested from the judicial vicars of each of the five Australian ecclesiastical tribunals. Replies were received from the judicial vicars of Adelaide, Melbourne, Perth and Sydney, all of whom asserted that there had never been a canonical penal trial of a cleric for CSA in their tribunal or any other. See Rev. Dr K. Matthews (SA/NT) to Jones, 5 February 2014; Very Rev. Prof. I. Waters (VIC/Tas) to Jones, 13 December 2013; Fr P. Blayney (NSW/ACT) to Jones, 18 December 2013; and Mons. M. Keating DCL (WA) to Jones, 20 December 2013, all in author's possession.

[36] Beal John, Coriden James and Green Thomas *New Commentary on the Code of Canon Law* Paulist Press New York 2000 p 1532.

were in effect choosing to impose temporary remedial, rather than permanent, penalties on priests guilty of child sex offences.[37]

Judicial proceedings are the only avenue of response in canon law that allowed bishops to impose permanent penalties on clergy found guilty of child sex offences. Australian bishops' decisions not to initiate judicial proceedings for clergy subject to credible allegations of child sexual abuse within the prescribed period can be interpreted in two ways. It might indicate that they were adhering to canonical process, but that they judged that a temporary administrative penalty, or fraternal correction or pastoral solicitude was sufficient to 'repair the scandal, restore justice, [and] reform the offender'.[38] On the other hand, the absence of judicial proceedings could indicate that bishops were not complying with canonical legal processes. Such non-compliance could indicate negligence, or a resort to non-canonical responses in the interest of effecting more expedient action.

Canonists and commentators on the Catholic Church are divided as to why the law, which so clearly regards child sex crimes as grave offences, was rarely used to impose substantive penalties on offending clergy. Some have opined that the current scandal could have been avoided if bishops had simply applied existing church law.[39] Pope Benedict XVI explicitly stated this in a letter to the Irish Catholic Church after the publication of the Ryan Report into child abuse in Irish institutions. He wrote that concern for the reputation of the Church and the avoidance of scandal resulted in a 'failure to apply existing canonical penalties'.[40] Others have argued that canon law was unwieldy, cumbersome and ultimately useless as a means of dealing with clerical child sexual abuse.[41]

Systemic issues in canon law have inhibited its capacity to discipline clergy. These include the five-year prescription period (similar to a statute of limitations), high standards of proof ('moral certainty') and the peculiar canonical principle of imputability. Imputability, or responsibility for action, states that 'those who habitually lack the use of reason are considered to be incapable of a delict, even if they violated a law or precept while seemingly sane'.[42] In a canonical penal trial if paedophilia was accepted as a mental disorder that limited a cleric's responsibility for his actions, persons found

[37] If bishops were proceeding canonically there would be an archival record, as records of preliminary investigations and administrative acts must be in writing (CIC83 cann 37 and 1719). It is possible that bishops may have acted out of expediency in ways that did not leave an archival record.

[38] CIC83 cann 1341 and 1718.

[39] Coughlin John 'The Clergy Sexual Abuse Crisis and the Spirit of Canon Law' (2003) 44 (4) *Boston College Law Review* 977; Pallone Nathaniel 'Sin, Crime, Arrogance, Betrayal: A Psychodynamic Perspective on the Crisis in American Catholicism' (2002) 2 (4) *Brief Treatment and Crisis Intervention* 341.

[40] Pope Benedict XVI 'Pastoral Letter of the Holy Father Pope Benedict XVI to the Catholics of Ireland', 19 March 2010, paragraph 4. Available at <http://www.vatican.va/holy_father/benedict_xvi/letters/2010/documents/hf_ben-xvi_let_20100319_church-ireland_en.html> Accessed 20 January 2014.

[41] Parkinson Patrick 'Child Sexual Abuse and the Churches: A Story of Moral Failure?' (2013) 13 (78) Sydney Law School Research Paper; Cafardi Nicolas *Before Dallas: The U.S. Bishops' Response to Clergy Sexual Abuse of Children* Paulist Press Mahwah 2008; Tapsell Keiran *Potiphar's Wife: The Vatican's Secret and Child Sexual Abuse* ATF Press Adelaide 2014.

[42] CIC83 can 1322.

guilty of sex crimes with the very young would not be able to receive the maximum penalty of dismissal from the clerical state. Many of these limitations were ameliorated in the instruction, *Crimen sollicitationis* (1922, 1962), however there has been considerable confusion about the adequacy of the instruction's publication and its applicability after the promulgation of the new Code of Canon Law in 1983.[43] On balance, although there were problems with the law, it is instructive to note that it was only after bishops in Ireland and the USA began to initiate trials in the 1990s that it has begun to function at least partially.

This history demonstrates that for the Roman Catholic Church, failures to respond appropriately to allegations of the sexual assault of children by clergy are not due to silences in canon law. For while it may have functioned imperfectly, canon law provided the Church with a way to recognise child sex crimes as particularly grave crimes, requiring a serious penal response. In fact, the testimony of canon law as to the gravity of clerical child sex offences is unambiguous, and was restated throughout this period. Yet, until very recently, the Church was in a state of denial regarding the significance of clerical sex offences. While in Australia there has never been a canonical trial of a priest for child sex crimes, from at least the 1960s Catholic sex offenders were referred for psychological treatment, and in 1997 the Australian Catholic Church also founded a clinical treatment centre for clerical sex offenders, Encompass Australasia. It treated over 1100 clergy, both Catholic and Protestant, before closing in 2008. This response, focusing on the redemption of the offender, amounts to what Cohen termed a state of implicatory denial: a failure to attend to the criminality of the acts and the harms experienced by victim/survivors of abuse.

4.0 Case Study Two: Governance in the Church of England, 1870–1970

In my second case study, this relationship between canon law and denial is reversed. This reversal is surprising, as the Church of England has a similar structure of government — episcopal — and a canon law tradition in common with the Roman Catholic Church. In addition, as the established Church of England, its law is passed through the Westminster Parliament. Unlike the Roman Catholic Church in Australia, it did utilise its ecclesiastical courts for the discipline of clergy for a range of offences, including sexual offences (incontinence) but also for drunkenness, financial impropriety, brawling, liturgical, doctrinal and various other offences. Research in the records of the Court of Arches, the Ecclesiastical court of appeal for the province of Canterbury, produced numerous examples of clergy disciplined through canonical processes (including for keeping prostitutes in the manse, writing erotic fantasies, and sexually assaulting domestic servants). As I have discussed elsewhere, for a variety of legal and historical reasons, there is little evidence of clergy subject to allegations of the sexual assault of children being tried through ecclesiastical courts.[44] One of the

[43] Beal John P 'The 1962 Instruction *Crimen sollicitationis:* Caught Red-Handed or Handed a Red Herring' (2007) 41 *Studia Canonica* 199.

[44] Jones Timothy 'Finding Child Sex Abuse in the Archives: The Treatment of Sexually Offending Clergy in the Church of England, 1871–1960' in Smaal Yorick, Finane Mark and Kaladelfos Amanda (eds) *The Sexual Abuse of Children* Monash University Press Melbourne forthcoming 2015.

major reasons for this is that, unlike in Roman Catholic canon law, age differentials do not feature as a significant descriptor in church records of sexual offences prior to 1970. While Anglican law and legal processes appear to have largely silenced age as a factor in categorising sexual offences in this period, records of the bishops' informal surveillance and governance of clergy reveal that this silence did not equate to a state of denial regarding clerical offending.

From 1871, Anglican bishops from England, Wales and Scotland met biannually or triannually in what was called the Bishops' Meeting. This was a secret, advisory meeting at which matters of common concern were discussed. A standing item in the minutes of the meeting was the maintenance of a 'cautionary list'. The list contained names of clergy who had committed an offence against their office. It was compiled and updated at the meeting and circulated to diocesan bishops for their information.[45] It was repeatedly emphasised that the Archbishop, who managed the list, 'was not in any sense a court which either pronounced or remitted sentences'.[46] The list was purely for the advice of the bishops and had no formal authority. A bishop was at liberty to appoint whomever he wanted, but should consult the list before making any appointment. It was frequently recorded in the minutes that the very existence of the list should not be known outside the bishops' meeting.[47]

The offences for which a cleric could be placed on the list varied greatly and, as with ecclesiastical court records, age is not a significant analytic category for sexual offences. Offences mentioned in the period varied from drunkenness, drug addiction, misappropriation of church funds, adultery, bigamy, remarriage after divorce,[48] the marriage of a clergyman to his deceased wife's sister, unnamed immorality, the capacious category of 'unnatural offences' and offences 'calculated to bring scandal on the Church'.[49] Clergy on the list were marked either 'C' or 'P'. Clergy marked 'C' had committed a lesser offence, and 'caution and enquiry' were advised before a person marked 'C' was allowed to officiate.[50] A cleric marked 'P', on the other hand, had committed a more serious offence. As Archbishop Lang stressed in 1941, 'those with entry "P" against their names ought in no circumstances to be in any way employed without consultation with the Archbishop of the Province'.[51] Names were not left on the list in perpetuity. The bishops regularly revised the list, adding names of new offenders, and removing names of men who had died, or 'where the nature of the caution deserved reconsideration'.[52]

[45] Although in 1947 for the first time an 'Advisory Council on the Treatment of Offenders' is mentioned, and bishops nominated to it. It is not clear from the minutes whether this was an ecclesiastic or secular body. Lambeth Palace Library, London, Archbishops' Archives, Bishops' Meetings Records [hereafter BM] vol 12 13–14/10/1947 p 168.

[46] BM vol 11 15/1/1940 p 62.

[47] BM vol 11 30/6–1/7/1941 p 131. The fact that this was repeated suggests that bishops did not keep it secret, and perhaps used it, or the threat of it, in their dealings with errant clergy.

[48] But not necessarily for getting divorced (BM vol 13 2–3/7/1951 p 29; BM vol 14 20–21/1/1959 p 239), nor for conducting the marriage of divorcees (BM vol 12 12/10/1948 p 12).

[49] BM vol 12 14/4/1945 p 2.

[50] Davidson Papers. Davidson Randall Thomas (1848–1930) Baron Davidson Archbishops' Papers Lambeth Palace Library London Archbishops' Archives 300 f 16.

[51] BM vol 11 30/6–1/7/1941 p 131.

[52] As above 15/1/1939 p 9.

While the bishops display an awareness of the law and their legal responsibilities and liabilities throughout the period, criminal justice responses to clerical offenders are not prominent in the archive. The bishops received legal advice in relation to offending clergy, including from the presiding judge of the Court of Arches.[53] In 1925, mindful of the potential legal harm to which confession might expose clergy, Archbishop Davidson:

> warned the younger bishops as to the peril of allowing incriminated clergy to make confession of wrong-doing to them without first insisting on an explicit understanding that the Bishop would not be bound to silence with regard to what was in such circumstances told to him.[54]

It was also proposed that on the repeated confession of 'sin of special gravity involving others', a condition of absolution should be that the priest:

> be willing to acknowledge [his] sin openly to his bishop and take the consequences: provided always that the bishop ought in dealing with any such penitent to have regard solely to what would best conduce to his spiritual restoration.[55]

The minutes include instances where the bishops gave evidence over to police to aid in the prosecution of clergy.[56] The caution list also indicates some cases where men had been included following their conviction of offences in state courts.

Even in cases that obviously involved minors, age does not feature as a category for understanding clerical sex offences in this archive. There is, however, voluminous discussion of the broader category of clerical homosexual offences. As will become evident, the techniques of surveillance and discipline developed to respond to clergy guilty of homosexual offences were similarly applied to child sex offenders. From the 1920s, bishops were particularly concerned by the apparent growth in homosexuality amongst the clergy. In reports published in 1929, 1945 and 1955, the bishops developed a strict attitude to clerical sex offenders. The 1929 report recommended that men guilty of homosexual offences should not be ordained, or allowed to continue in ministry.[57] This finding was repeated by the 1945 report, which recommended that 'the proof or admission of a homosexual crime committed by a clerk in holy Orders shall involve his final and irrecoverable deposition from such Orders'.[58] Homosexuality, per se, was not grounds for deposition, but the commission of homosexual conduct punishable

[53] BM vol 8 21–2/5/1924 p 29. The Dean of the Arches is the judge who sits at the ecclesiastical court of the Archbishop of Canterbury. It is a joint appointment to the equivalent Chancery Court in the archdiocese of York.

[54] BM vol 8 8–9/7/1925 p 61. There was also discussion of bishops' liability for legal expenses when dealing with offending clergy. See: BM vol 13 8–9/7/1952 p 178.

[55] BM vol 12 14/4/1945.

[56] Although none of these cases involved child sex offences: BM vol 12 11/1/1950 p 333; BM vol 14 17–18/1/1955 p 3; BM vol 14 18–19/10/1955 p 26.

[57] The Archbishops' Committee on Spiritual Healing. Second Interim Report. Report on Homosexuality in Relation to the Ministry of the Church. 11 July 1929. BM vol 9 p 261–2.

[58] Report of the Episcopal Committee on Discipline, BM vol 12 p 16–17.

by the law, 'ought to be held to constitute a permanent disqualification for any further exercise of ministry, in any circumstance, in the Church'.[59]

The archives show that, like Roman Catholic bishops, Anglican bishops frequently resorted to medical advice and treatment for sex offenders. The relationship between medicine and the church was evident throughout the period, though it was not always smooth. Archbishop Davidson, for example:

> mentioned the difficult position in which he was placed when psychotherapeutists minimized the responsibility of clergymen who had committed immorality and suggested that the cure of these men depended at least in part on their being allowed to continue at work.[60]

On the whole, it appears that the bishops valued medical advice highly. In the mid-twentieth century medics were involved in the selection and training of ordinands, and bishops were warned of 'the danger of ordaining a psychopathic man'.[61] In discussions of confession and the discipline of the clergy frequent reference was made to the value of expert and psychiatric help.[62] In the 1950s a list was maintained of 'institutions and of individual psychiatrists skilled in dealing with homosexuals'.[63] Archbishop Fisher remarked that it was his personal practice to send men in his diocese under discipline for sexual offences to a psychiatrist and ask for a full report.[64] Throughout the period they explicitly framed sexual offences in terms of sex, crime and disease.[65] In the 1955 'Memorandum on Homosexuals' it was remarked that homosexuality was unlike 'other psychological maladjustments on which doctors report, as it is in fact widely regarded as a moral defect, and as the law stands lays a man open to suspicion of a crime'.[66] The 1945 Episcopal Committee on Discipline report was written by three bishops, and advised by Dr E.A.H. Pentreath of the Mickleover Mental Hospital, Derbyshire and Mr Justice Vaisey. The recognition of homosexuality as a medical condition without cure in this report meant that clergy guilty of homosexual offences could not be reinstated. This was not regarded as a penalty, but 'as a necessary protection of the Church against a moral risk too serious to be rightfully taken ... no exceptions ought to be made to the application of this principle'.[67] It was recommended that clergy deposed for these reasons should be helped spiritually, financially and psychologically, possibly through the newly inaugurated services of the NHS.[68]

---

59 As above.
60 BM vol 8 26–7/5/1925 p 75.
61 BM vol 12 11/10/1949 p 305.
62 BM vol 11 9–10/10/1944 p 392–5.
63 BM vol 14 18–19/10/1955 p 35.
64 As above.
65 See: The Archbishops' Committee on Spiritual Healing. Second Interim Report. Report on Homosexuality in Relation to the Ministry of the Church. 11 July 1929. BM vol 9 p 261–2; and Report of the Episcopal Committee on Discipline, BM vol 12 p 16–17.
66 Report No. 5. Central Advisory Council on Training for the Ministry: Memorandum on Homosexuals'. BM vol 14 Appendix.
67 BM vol 12 p 16–17.
68 As above.

In addition to referring men to secular psychological and psychiatric services, the Church treated men under discipline for sexual and other offences directly through a number of in-house channels. In 1924 the bishops discussed what was to be done with clergy guilty of 'unnatural offences'. Archbishop Davidson remarked that the problem of these 'black sheep' was terrible, and that he had been examining how the Roman Catholics dealt with them.[69] Archbishop Lang observed that their segregation in 'Homes' would be undesirable, and suggested that they could be billeted out to clergy with large vicarages. By 1932, they had an established a method of dealing with clerical offenders which operated at least for the next 30 years. Men with drug or alcohol addiction were referred to Caldecote Hall, a Church of England Temperance Society retreat in Warwickshire. Most clerical sexual offenders and clergy disciplined for other serious offences were sent to be cared for and rehabilitated by officers of the Church Army. The Church Army was founded in 1882 as an evangelistic and social work organisation within the Church. It provided spiritual guidance as well as material care for clerics and their families. These treatment avenues were reviewed periodically, particularly when the Church Army officer responsible for clerical offenders retired. One such discussion in 1955 is revealing of the limits of their practice. Bishop Mortimer of Exeter explained that on coming out of prison, clerics guilty of homosexual offences 'went for a period to a Religious Community, after which they worked in a parish on probation'.[70] He lamented that 'all too frequently these men broke down again, because they had received no real curative treatment, and suggested that such men should not be allowed to officiate again, or 'alternatively that a residential centre should be established for these priests where psychiatric treatment could be given to them'.[71] The Primus of Scotland, Thomas Hannay, similarly criticised the placement of men in religious communities because of the lack of available psychiatric help there. Nevertheless, the bishops regarded that a dedicated treatment centre would be too expensive, and continued sending men to the Church Army for supervision, rehabilitation and care.

While age is not a significant analytic category in the bishops' discussions of clerical offenders, this archival silence does not equate to an absence of evidence of offences against children. From handwritten annotations on a draft revision of the cautionary list from 1903, it is evident that at least 13% of annotated offenders had offended against children.[72] Similarly, a closer reading of their discussions of homosexual offences reveals that offences against boys — possibly the most numerous of child sex offences — were submerged in this category. This different taxonomy is seen most clearly in correspondence between the bishops and the Boy Scouts Association. In 1947 the bishops instituted procedures to be followed for 'clerical scouters who had been convicted of offence, or whose behaviour is indiscrete, foolish or unsuitable'.[73] They were to have their warrants as scouting officers refused, and their diocesan bishops were to be informed. There was continuing correspondence between the Scouts and the bishops on the issue. The Scouts asked for assurances that 'before allowing a priest to resume

[69] BM vol 8 21–2/5/1924 p 29.
[70] BM vol 1 18–19/10/1955 p 35.
[71] As above.
[72] Above note 32.
[73] BM vol 12 14/1/1947 p 128–9.

his ministry after an offence the Bishop concerned would require an undertaking that he would not apply for or accept any position in the Scout Movement' and nominate someone else to manage the scouts in his parish.[74] Launcelot Fleming, the Bishop of Portsmouth, noted that 'Scout policy was that the police should be at once informed' if offences against boys were suspected. They 'did not feel that any exception to this could be made in the case of a clergyman'.[75] In 1956 and 1957 the bishops further tightened their regulation of clerical scout masters by making the appointment of clergy to scouting positions an episcopal responsibility. This meant that bishops could check the cautionary list, thereby 'never approving the appointment of any clergyman who at any time was known to be guilty of homosexual misconduct'.[76] Even in this very obvious case of child sex abuse, the offences were categorised as 'homosexual misconduct'. The silencing of age in Anglican bishops' governance of sex offenders through euphemism and the categorisation of offences through sex and sexuality, might thus equate to what Cohen termed 'interpretive denial': not a denial that offences took place, but that they involved children. This, however, does not seem to have led to the level of implicatory denial operative in the Catholic Church. Anglican bishops did act to surveil, discipline and treat clerical child sex offenders.

5.0 Conclusion

These two case studies do not overturn the uncomfortable concurrence between feminist, historians of sexuality and Church authorities on the 'late' 're-discovery' of child sexual abuse. They remind us, however, that churches have their own law, which has operated over time to both deny and recognise clerical sex offenders, and to mete punishment and maintain surveillance. An analysis of the different silences in the history of canon law and governance complicates narratives of the late 'discovery' of CSA. Attending to the ways that sex with minors was conceived prior to the feminist formulation of 'Child Sex Abuse' as a particular phenomenon in the late twentieth century reveals different possibilities of denial or acknowledgement.

Ironically, the Roman Catholic provisions of celibacy for its clergy provided the clearest framework for the acknowledgement of the gravity of child sex offences in Catholic canon law. Child sex offences are unambiguously listed amongst the most grave offences that canon law recognises. And this was repeated throughout the twentieth century, including most clearly in the 1983 code of canon law, which was promulgated on the eve of the child sex abuse crisis breaking in the United States. The contrast between the unambiguous testimony of the Church's canon law to the harms of CSA, and the Church's neglect of this law in the twentieth century could not be more striking. This disjuncture perhaps explains the less credible, more strenuous forms of denial exhibited at recent inquiries by Catholic authorities.

The legal formulations of the Church of England, on the other hand, are not as clear as to the specific harms of child sex offences. Yet, the remarkable (intentional

[74] As above 5–6/7/1954 p 354.

[75] As above. Archbishop Fisher noted that these arrangements had been in place since 1947 but were not needed until 1952.

[76] BM vol 12 16–17/10/1956 p 79.

or unknowing) openness of the Church's archives for the nineteenth century to the 1960s provides a window into the ways in which child sex offenders were treated by the Church. This is not a straightforward reading. Yet, by following established feminist methods of combating archival silences (in this case reading the bishops' treatment of all kinds of clerical offenders) it is possible to construct a general picture of how clerical child sex offenders were treated by church authorities.[77]

The primary form of treatment, well established by the late nineteenth century, was the surveillance of offending clergy through the maintenance and circulation amongst the bishops of a cautionary list. The cautionary list enabled bishops not to appoint, or to restrict the duties, of men guilty of serious offences. A key purpose of the list was to prevent men banned in one diocese from moving to another area to gain employment. Men guilty of sexual offences were commonly deposed from office, or prohibited from exercising duties for a period of five years or more. Throughout the period psychological and psychiatric advice and treatment was indicated. From at least 1932, bishops referred sexual offenders to officers of the Church Army who assisted in their rehabilitation. This could include assistance with housing, employment and psychological treatment. The bishops also cooperated with the legal prosecution of offenders, although in all treatments the bishops were 'to have regard solely to what would best conduce to [the penitent's] spiritual restoration'.[78] As with their Catholic equivalents, Anglican bishops' first consideration in their treatment of clergy was for the salvation and rehabilitation of the offenders, and for the wider reputation and mission of the Church. In what has become a tragically familiar absence, there is no mention in this archive of their care or responsibility for survivors of clerical abuse. The offender is acknowledged, but the harms of their offences experienced by survivors are silenced.

These historical cases confirm what existing research has shown, that from the 1970s and particularly the 1980s there was a reinvigorated interest and concern with child sex offences. But they also show that prior to the feminist articulation of sexual politics and sexual violence as a wider social and political issue, there were frameworks for the recognition of the gravity and harm of these offences. As Carol Smart observed 15 years ago, 'following Foucault, we should cease to see this under-researched era in the history of child sexual abuse merely as a period of silence and more as a moment of immense verbosity'.[79] Just because it was almost universally neglected, it does not mean that Roman Catholic canon law did not contain a framework within which to recognise the harms of CSA. And just because, in the Anglican Church, child sex offences were not named as such, it does not mean that they were not being dealt with. Common to both case studies, however, are techniques of interpretative and implicatory denial that limited and contained responses to clerical CSA to the rehabilitation of the offender, neglecting pastoral care and justice for survivors.

[77] Allen Judith 'Evidence and Silence: Feminism and the Limits of History' in Pateman Carole and Gross Elizabeth (eds) *Feminist Challenges: Social and Political Theory* Allen & Unwin Sydney1986 p 173.

[78] BM vol 12 11/1/1950 p 333.

[79] Smart (2000) above note 22 at 69.

Reparation for Betrayal of Trust in Child Sexual Abuse Cases: The Christian Duty of Care, Vicarious Liability and the Church of England

Kim Stevenson, Judith Rowbotham and Jason Lowther

Abstract. Feminist challenges to the traditional principles of vicarious liability highlight the difficulties facing claimants seeking redress via a doctrine largely developed in relation to the corporate model reflecting masculine traits of institutional power and control embedded in the traditional enterprise employer/employee relationship. This article explores the ways in which the recent spate of claims made against UK religious authorities regarding present and historic acts of child sexual abuse perpetrated by clergy have forced a paradigm shift requiring the courts to consider influences on the legal process associated with tropes of restorative justice, powerfully supported and explained by feminist legal theorists. The position of the Roman Catholic Church, however, is shown to be very different to that of the Church of England, highlighting the need for the paradigm shift to develop further and to consider the role of validation and vindication as elements in reparation, institutional as well as individual.

1.0 Introduction

Accusations of child sexual abuse perpetrated by figures of religious authority have become public over the past three decades in England. Initially focus was on the Roman Catholic Church but the revelations have increasingly included Protestant denominations. The accusations made in respect of Roman Catholic clergy precipitated a number of complex civil claims against their respective 'employers'. In turn this highlighted powerful challenges, particularly from feminist perspectives, to existing thought on tort doctrine and remedies. Notably, these have included ideas relating to restorative justice approaches.[1] Judgments have revealed considerable movement in legal guidelines in relation to vicarious liability and limitation periods. The UK courts

[1] Encapsulated in Strang Heather and Braithwaite John (eds) *Restorative Justice and Family Violence* Cambridge University Press Cambridge 2002.

have now established in principle that the Roman Catholic Church has responsibility for its priests as 'employees', but this has not yet been successfully extended to the Protestant churches in England, despite the official acceptance by various churches of extensive incidents of historical child sexual abuse practised by some of their priests.

Reparative gestures have been made by the Church of England, including a public apology from the Archbishop of Canterbury, Justin Welby, endorsed by the Synod.[2] But official church guidelines do not reference any form of reparation to match the levels of remorse expressed other than offers of spiritual support. The issue explored by this article is what this acceptance of moral responsibility actually means in terms of the legal liability of the Anglican Church for English claimants. This has wider implications for other Protestant churches.[3] The current situation regarding the Church of England raises the question of what the priorities are in respect of victims of such abuse when seeking vindication and associated reparation.[4] Does (can) the traditional remedy of financial compensation proffer sufficient reparation? The need for harm vindication, expressed through strategies such as the public 'validatory' airing of the less tangible (and quantifiable) consequences of abuse claims via the court system, has been central to the challenges to legal thought posed by feminist scholars like Kathleen Daly.[5] The recent overturning by an Independent Review of the Director of Public Prosecutions' decision not to prosecute Lord Janner on historic child sexual abuse charges suggests that the legal and political establishment are responding to these, but what of the churches?[6] In line with harm vindication principles, public apologies are being freely offered by the churches but can apology alone ever be a sufficient reparative response?[7] This discussion utilises feminist legal theory to reflect on the responsibility of these spiritual institutions with specific reference to claims of vicarious liability as the primary civil law mechanism for holding organisations to account.

2.0 Synthesising Feminist Legal Theory and Vicarious Liability

For over 20 years, feminist scholars, including Leslie Bender, Patricia Peppin and Josephine Donovan, have argued that the application of tortious principles, traditionally presented as 'neutral and unbiased', should properly take into account issues

[2] 'Child Abuse Apology from Church of England' *Christian Today* 7 July 2013 <http://www.christiantoday.com/article/child.abuse.apology.from.church.of.england/33106.htm> Accessed 13 July 2015.

[3] This includes the Church in Wales, and the Church of Scotland. While Anglican, neither are state nor established churches so their legal position is different to that of the Anglican Church in England itself.

[4] Varuhas Jason 'The Concept of "Vindication" in the Law of Torts: Rights, Interests and Damages' (2014) 34 (2) *Oxford Journal of Legal Studies* 253.

[5] Daly Kathleen 'Sexual Assault and Restorative Justice' in Strang and Brathwaite (eds) *Restorative Justice* above note 1.

[6] Former Labour MP and member of the House of Lords diagnosed with Alzheimer's Disease: 'Lord Janner to be Prosecuted for Child Sex Offences' *Daily Telegraph* 30 June 2015 <http://www.telegraph.co.uk/news/uknews/crime/11705439/Lord-Janner-to-be-prosecuted-for-child-sex-offences.html> Accessed 13 July 2015.

[7] Smith Nick *Justice Through Apologies: Remorse, Reform and Punishment* Cambridge University Press Cambridge 2014.

highlighted by wider feminist perspectives including the implications of the inherent language of law for justice delivery.[8] Peppin claims that the fundamental negligence concepts of harm, duty and standard of care 'need to be construed in a manner sensitive to historic disadvantage'.[9] Since the typically masculine traits of hierarchy and dominance both 'disadvantage [and] characterise relationships in life', then a corresponding 'awareness of this dimension should enter into the determination of liability and compensation'.[10] Bender argues:

> Tort law needs to be more of a system of response and caring ... Its focus should be on interdependence and collective responsibility rather than on individuality, and on safety and help for the injured rather than on 'reasonableness' and economic efficiency.[11]

Her espousal of the concept of '*re*tort' is illuminating, partly as in the sense of a conversational response to legal theory and judicial practice; but also as a theoretical device, to reconceptualise and reconstruct the application of tortious liability through feminist legal method.[12] Like Daly, Bender insists that a full remedy of harms would require consideration of the 'physical, emotional, and interpersonal losses or "costs" inflicted upon particular individuals, and the continued, dangerous decision making potential of the errant corporation'.[13] In other words, if it is to fulfil its supposed legal function, which includes as strategic aims both deterrence and compensation, tort law must recognise emotional, physical and spiritual harms. Along with Daly's framing reflections on harm vindication and the need for validation in achieving justice, Bender's groundbreaking, and in the context of sexual abuse claims, prescient, feminist critique of tort law provides the basis for our subsequent focus on what has been achieved, and what challenges remain. Her critical themes of equality, responsibility, remedy and alternative legal strategies are also employed to reflect on the extent to which judicial reasoning in the leading cases reviewed here relates to the challenges posed by such critiques.[14]

For Carol Gilligan as well as Daly, questions of morality from a feminist perspective focus upon 'context ... relationships, equity, and responsibility'; with interconnectedness as a defining characteristic of a relationship rather than the quintessentially hierarchical conceptualisations of more conventional male perspectives.[15] Furthermore, tortious remedies should not be limited to financial

---

[8] See Bender Leslie 'A Lawyer's Primer on Feminist Theory and Tort' (1998) 38 *Journal of Legal Education* 3; 'Feminist (Re)torts: Thoughts on the Liability Crisis, Mass Torts, Power, and Responsibilities' (1990) *Duke Law Journ*al 848; Peppin Patricia 'A Feminist Challenge to Tort Law' in Bottomley Anne (ed.) *Feminist Perspectives on the Foundational Subjects of Law* Cavendish London 1996 p 69. Donovan Josephine *Feminist Theory: The Intellectual Traditions* 3rd edition Continuum New York 2006.

[9] Peppin as above at 70.

[10] As above.

[11] Bender 'A Lawyer's Primer' above note 8 at 4.

[12] Bender 'Feminist (Re)torts' above note 8 at 865.

[13] Daly above note 5 at 36.

[14] Bender 'A Lawyer's Primer' above note 8.

[15] Gilligan Carol *In a Different Voice: Psychological Theory and Women's Development* Cambridge Massachusetts 1982 cited in Bender 'A Lawyer's Primer' above note 8 at 3.

compensation but should recognise and accommodate other means of reparation; something which could include public acknowledgement of instances of abuse, via court hearings, as well as apologies. As Conaghan has commented, 'over the last few decades feminists have been at the vanguard of boundary changes to tort liability, particularly in relation to claims deriving from sexual … harm'.[16] Certainly the criticisms in such scholarship are fundamental to understanding the implications of changes in the practices in the English courts in the last quarter-century, particularly in the re-visitation of vicarious liability in recent judicial reasoning in relation to the Roman Catholic Church. But the question remains of where this leaves the Church of England.

Under the Salmond Test, vicarious liability is a device whereby a party may become liable for the tort of another. Strictly speaking both parties remain defendants, although for practical purposes, usually related to the ability of one (deeper pocket) defendant to assume liability, there will be only one party held liable.[17] The traditional doctrinal approach was to locate that arrangement within a defined employment, or *master and servant*, relationship. Society and the law have moved beyond such linguistic and conceptual antiquity, preferring a contemporary reading of vicarious liability. This involves reconsideration of the extent of the connections that cement the relationship between the two defendants; the actual tortfeasor and the legal person deemed responsible.[18]

3.0 Vicarious Liability in the Context of Clergy Abuse

The traditional perspective effectively debarred such judicial consideration until the leading judgment in *Caparo* in 1990, which imported notions of 'fairness' and 'justice' to accompany the 'reasonable' when determining the existence of a general duty of care, with the implications that had for vicarious liability.[19] The broadening of the Salmond Test, identified from the start as imprecise and necessarily requiring pragmatism,[20] provides the first evidence of a shift from the traditional doctrinal straitjacketing towards justice mechanisms more in line with harm vindication concepts. A decade later, this underpinned the House of Lords' judgment in *Lister v Hesley Hall* in 2001. Lord Millet held that 'an employer who is not personally at fault is made legally answerable for the fault of his employee' where an inextricable

[16] Foreword by Conaghan Joanne in Richardson Janice and Rackley Erica (eds) *Feminist Perspectives on Tort Law* Routledge Abingdon 2012 p iv.

[17] The test was formulated by Sir John William Salmond, in his *Law of Torts: A Treatise on the English Law of Liability for Civil Injuries* (1907): 'a master is not responsible for a wrongful act done by his servant unless it is done in the course of his employment. It is deemed to be so done if it is either (1) a wrongful act authorised by the master, or (2) a wrongful and unauthorised act mode of doing some act authorised by the master.' at 83-84. The test was applied by Salmond LJ in e.g. *Morris v C W Martin & Sons* [1966] 1 QB 716, at para 738. Most often this is seen in an employment relationship, in which circumstance it is usual for the employer to be required to obtain third party liability insurance.

[18] For a discussion of this evolution see the judgment of Ward LJ in *JGE v The Trustees of the Portsmouth Roman Catholic Diocesan Trust* [2013] QB 722; [2012] EWCA Civ 938 paras 19–72.

[19] *Caparo Industries plc v Dickman* [1990] 2 AC 605; [1990] UKHL 2 (per Lord Bridge at 5).

[20] As above.

link could be established between wrongful acts and the employment involved, in this case, sexual abuse of children by school staff.[21] Recent UK Supreme Court and Court of Appeal decisions dealing with abuse claims against the clergy suggest that the judiciary are regularly exhibiting the levels of awareness highlighted by Peppin in relation to cases involving the Roman Catholic Church. This has included a more generous interpretation of vicarious liability targeting those with the means to finance compensation for victim claimants. It ensures that if an 'employer' has created risk through, broadly, an employment relationship, they should be expected to be vicariously liable if that risk transpires.[22] Per Lord Phillips in the *Catholic Child Welfare* case, 'it is fair, just and reasonable' for vicarious liability to be shared with the employing school by an institute of the Catholic Church, given that the abuse was committed by Catholic monks.[23] In the context of the emphasis elsewhere on restorative justice in the last quarter-century, a greater willingness of victims to come forward in these cases has manifested itself. This has enabled courts to make a paradigm shift where contextual factors identified as crucial to a vindication of hurt felt and indicative of a betrayal of the duty of care are positively considered when applying the principles of vicarious liability.[24] Such broadening of responsibility would not necessarily have been achieved but for the framing factor provided by the distinctive factors presented in these cases, alongside the non-corporate structure of religious institutions and the relatively uncomplicated legal nature of the non-established Roman Catholic Church in the UK.[25]

This contrasts with the complexities surrounding the legal position of the established Church of England. It leaves it open to question how far, in practice, the redrawn vicarious liability concept can be utilised successfully to deal with all cases involving clerical sexual abuse of children. The failure, to date, to bring any case against the Church of England as an institution, despite a number of convictions of individual clergy on abuse charges,[26] suggests that a sole reliance on the vicarious liability doctrine may not be sufficient to permit the delivery of what victims would see as 'justice' and an appropriate recompense for the harm done to them.

Despite the advances noted, an essentially traditional fixation on monetary compensation as the principal remedy for harm continues to dominate. In practice, in most instances where tortious liability is proven, financial compensation is the inevitable outcome as opposed to other forms of 'corrective justice'.[27] But Honore argues that a tortfeasor's accountability as an 'outcome responsibility' is broader than any moral blame or legal liability and one that 'figures prominently in our sense of our own agency and is important for both the theory of agency and moral

[21] *Lister v Hesley Hall* [2002] 1 AC 215.

[22] See *A v Archbishop of Birmingham* [2005] EWHC 1361 (QB); *Maga v The Trustees of the Birmingham Archdiocese of the Roman Catholic Church* [2010] EWCA Civ 85.

[23] *Catholic Child Welfare Society v Various claimants* [2013] 2 AC 1; [2012] UKSC 56, 94.

[24] Kalbian Aline *Sexing the Church, Gender, Power and Politics in Contemporary Catholicism* Indiana State University Press Bloomington 2005 p 139.

[25] It is recognised that this experience has not been shared in Australia, for instance.

[26] *R v Rideout* 20 May 2013 (unreported, Lewes Crown Court).

[27] See Beever Allan 'Corrective Justice and Personal Responsibility in Tort Law' (2008) 28 (3) *Oxford Journal of Legal Studies* 475.

theory'.[28] This could be used to challenge radically the issue of where responsibility lies in moral terms, thereby theoretically having the potential to make religious institutions, including the Church of England, consider to what extent moral responsibility should be practically recognised by them, especially given their avowed objective of working to repair the harm done to individuals in the Anglican communion by clerical abusers.[29]

4.0 Vicarious Liability and the Roman Catholic Church

In considering the peculiar legal position of the Church of England, a review of the development of the legal doctrine of vicarious liability in relation to the Roman Catholic Church needs to be undertaken to understand why the option of bringing such claims has not similarly been applied to the Church of England. When, in 1850, the Roman Catholic ecclesiastical hierarchy was re-established in the UK for the first time since the Reformation, care was taken to ensure that it was placed on a very different legal basis to the Church of England. The reasoning was to prevent any claims for restoration of ecclesiastical property, from churches to land, formerly in the possession of the Roman Catholic Church.[30] Consequently, in the late twentieth century, once individual perpetrators started to be convicted, lawyers who successfully brought civil claims on behalf of those abused against the Roman Catholic Church in England could not simply presume they would be able to replicate such claims against the Anglican Church.

In January 2012, Sean O'Neill, the Crime Editor at *The Times*, published a list of 31 named Roman Catholic priests convicted of child sex offences in the English courts between 2008 and 2011. In addition an unknown number received police cautions.[31] Disclosure of the scale of abuse was a factor in the willingness of concerned legal practitioners to pursue vicarious liability claims, not simply for financial recompense but as a way of achieving validatory public acknowledgment of harm done by institutions and their personnel with a moral as well as a secular duty of care. Richard Scorer, senior partner at Pannone LLP, is reported as stating that at any one time over 30 civil cases involving clerical abuse claims were being handled by lawyers. In Scorer's view the Roman Catholic Church's policies and procedures have improved since the 2001 Nolan Review on Child Protection in the Catholic Church in England and Wales.[32] However, he has cautioned that the full extent of the clerical abuse has yet to be uncovered, something he accounts for by reference to Canon 490 of the Code of Canon Law, which requires each bishop to maintain a secret and secure document

[28] Honore Tony *Responsibility and Fault* Hart Portland 1999 p 77.

[29] New Safeguarding and Clergy Discipline Measures will become law in 2016, after passing through Synod. See <http://www.itv.com/news/2015-04-07/dozens-of-historical-church-of-england-child-abuse-allegations-made/> Accessed 14 September 2015.

[30] Paz Denis *Popular Anti-Catholicism in Mid-Victorian England* University of Stanford Press Stanford 1992.

[31] O'Neill Sean 'Locked Archives that Guard the Catholic Church's Guilty Secrets' *The Times* 17 January 2012 p 8.

[32] Available at <http://www.cathcom.org/mysharedaccounts/cumberlege/finalnolan1.htm> Accessed 16 October 2015.

archive.[33] Also militating against the assumption that the Church is moving towards an acknowledgment of the need for reparation for abuse, as O'Neill highlights, compensation awards secured against the Catholic Church have been relatively small, typically £10,000–20,000. After all, the 'Church often deploys expensive lawyers and complex arguments to resist claims' in the courts, prioritising the maintenance of its assets over restorative justice to victims.[34]

A continuing preference for negotiated financial settlements before court hearings is disturbing given that victims are often less concerned about financial outcomes than with gaining a public airing for their claims through the courts, as a means of achieving validation to their sufferings. In 2004, former altar boy Simon Grey was the beneficiary of what is generally identified as the first substantive out of court settlement agreed by the Catholic Church in the UK. Abused between 1975 and 1981 by Father Christopher Clonan at Christ the King Church, Coventry, Grey brought proceedings against the Birmingham Archdiocese for breach of their duty of care. Just before the High Court hearing the Archdiocese offered £300,000 in settlement which Grey accepted. However, in subsequent media interviews, Grey made it clear that he felt he had not benefitted from harm vindication:

> I would have liked to have my case heard in open court, but pursuing that principle could have cost me money and my sanity. I suffered serious abuse and that was what this was about: my abuse and others' abuse.[35]

In 2005, though, Clonan's actions were finally exposed in the courts. The High Court in Manchester awarded £635,684 (the largest sum to date) to claimant A, who was abused by Clonan between 1977 and 1988, starting when A, the child of devoted Catholics who had welcomed Clonan into their home, was aged seven.[36] Implicitly acknowledging a quasi-restorative justice dimension to the case, Justice Clarke commented that as a regular visitor to the home Clonan was 'trusted and admired. The abuse was the grossest breach of the trust that A and his family had placed in him'.[37] As a child, A had not understood what was happening and then had become too scared to speak out, fearing he would not be believed. The judge's direct acknowledgement of harm done therefore amounted to an appropriate vindication accompanying the more traditional financial compensation.[38] Equally, the award was not challenged by the Church.

[33] O'Neill above note 31. See generally Scorer Richard '"Can I Sue the Pope?" Child Abuse Litigation Against the Holy See' (2012) *Journal of Personal Injury Law* 25; The Rt Hon The Lord Nolan, *Nolan Review on Child Protection in the Catholic Church in England and Wales* Report (2001); Code of Canon Law, c. 490, in *The Code of Canon Law: Latin-English Edition* Washington DC: Canon Law Society of America (1983).

[34] As above.

[35] 'Compensation for Former Altar Boy' *BBC News* 12 January 2004. <http://news.bbc.co.uk/2/hi/uk_news/england/west_midlands/3391103.stm> Accessed 23 February 2015.

[36] *A v Archbishop of Birmingham* [2005] EWHC 1361 (QB).

[37] As above paras 1–3.

[38] The sustained abuse caused schizophrenia and post-traumatic stress disorder which triggered the disclosure of the allegations at the age of 22; A was 35 years of age at the time of the hearing.

Belief that it had a positive impact on victims is supported by the fact that another of Clonan's victims came forward seeking validation via the courts.[39]

Clonan had paid Maga (an epileptic 12-year-old non-Catholic boy with severe learning difficulties) small sums of money for odd jobs and invited him to attend discos at the church. There he had been abused by Clonan in the presbytery. Represented by the Official Solicitor, Maga claimed the Trustees of the Birmingham Diocese were vicariously liable for Clonan's abuse and negligent in not following up a number of allegations, including one made in 1974 by the parents of another boy to Clonan's immediate supervisor, Father McTernan. The Trustees' response argued not only that the claim was time-barred but also that they were not vicariously liable as Clonan's actions were not 'closely connected' to his 'employment'. Lord Neuberger MR found common ground between the Church and other professions and corporate entities. Father Clonan normally dressed in his clerical 'uniform'. This denoted his position of trust and responsibility and intensified his moral authority. His 'duty' to evangelise extended to Catholics and non-Catholics alike; he was also given specifically assigned responsibility to engage with young people (grooming Maga under the guise of performing his pastoral duties) which:

> gave him the status and opportunity to draw the claimant further into his sexually abusive orbit by ostensibly respectable means connected with his employment as a priest at the Church.[40]

Ultimately, the Court of Appeal determined that the claim was not time-barred because of the ruling in *Hoare* (discussed below). More significantly, it confirmed for Maga that the abuse had in fact occurred, the Roman Catholic Church owed a duty of care to him and the other victims and it had been negligent in failing to supervise Father Clonan appropriately and not investigating the earlier complaints. The Church was therefore vicariously liable as the close connection test was established and there were sufficient additional factors that made it fair, just and reasonable to hold the Church to account.

5.0 Further Developments

In a further challenge to progressive reasoning, O'Sullivan has expressed concern that understandings of vicarious liability have been 'driven by unusual, extreme situations hovering around its edge, because only with a clearly defined edge can we be sure what forms the core of the rule'.[41] Her assertion that vicarious liability 'is being shaped and defined by cases involving child abuse, miles away from its bread and butter function of making commercial employers pay for the negligence of their employees' reveals an ongoing reluctance by some in the English court system to move vicarious liability thinking forward.[42] Fortunately, others accept that evolution of legal concepts and

[39] *Maga v The Trustees of the Birmingham Archdiocese* [2010] EWCA Civ 85 especially paras 45–50.
[40] As above at para 48.
[41] O'Sullivan Janet 'Case Comment: The Sins of the Father — Vicarious Liability Extended' (2012) *Cambridge Law Journal* 485.
[42] As above.

principles does depend upon boundary shifts, and a degree of flexibility to accommodate new realities. Concepts of 'employment' are usefully more fluid than in previous generations and provision of services increasingly exists outside normal commercial contexts. It is therefore appropriate that the law reflects the contemporary landscape. A close connection test potentially enables a positive outcome, in that a greater emphasis is placed on an 'employer' to ensure effective oversight or supervision of an employee.

This evolution of tort law is often a creation of policy factors and in that context the desirability of a 'clearly defined edge' was addressed in the Court of Appeal by Lord Justice Ward in *JGE v The Trustees of the Portsmouth Roman Catholic Diocesan Trust*. This laid the basis for a seminal Supreme Court decision later that year, *E v English Province of Our Lady of Charity.*[43] The claimant's case was that Father Wilfred Baldwin, appointed by the Portsmouth Diocese, raped her when she was seven years old and living in a Roman Catholic children's home run by an order of nuns. The defendants, Our Lady of Charity, were the order and trustees of a trust which had stood in the place of the diocesan bishop at the material time. The defendants claimed that their relationship with the priest was not analogous to an employer/employee relationship as there was no written employment contract. As priests were appointed verbally, the Bishop had no authority to supervise, only advise; no wages were paid by the diocese and priests could not be dismissed except by the Pope. While Father Baldwin owed the Bishop obedience he was free to conduct himself and his ministry as he wished and was only answerable to the canon law. Two of the judges at the Court of Appeal (Ward and Davis LLJ) held that there was a close connection between the tortfeasor and the defendant.[44] Their relationship was 'so close in character' to that of an employee and employer that it was 'just and fair' to hold the defendant liable because of the extent to which the priest was integrated into the structure of the Church and the centrality of his role. Ward concluded that vicarious liability is a fluid concept that needs to be determined in context.[45] Here, that context was the seriousness of the sexual abuse, which has 'emphatically moved beyond the confines of a contract of service'.[46] He stressed on more than one occasion that liability should only be fixed where it is 'just and fair' to hold the defendant vicariously liable tempering Kidner's clearly patriarchal tests which follow the orthodoxy of control, integration, organisation and entrepreneur.[47]

Ward concluded by briefly reviewing some of the main themes of vicarious liability: control, compensation, deterrence, loss-spreading and enterprise liability.[48] This echoes Bender in that it established a position that there is 'no single rationale that provides a complete answer for the imposition of vicarious liability' and that

[43] *JGE v The Trustees of the Portsmouth Roman Catholic Diocesan Trust* [2013] QB 722; [2012] EWCA Civ 938.
[44] As above at paras 81, 131.
[45] At paras 59–60.
[46] At para 73.
[47] At paras 70 and 72 citing Kidner Richard 'Vicarious Liability: For Whom Should the Employer be Liable?' (1995) 15 *Legal Studies* 47.
[48] At paras 74–81.

the courts rarely 'speak with one voice'.[49] On the one hand, his position reflects Fleming's *Law of Torts* that 'the modern doctrine of vicarious liability … should be frankly recognised in having its basis in a combination of policy considerations'.[50] It also reflects McLachlin CJ's comment in the Canadian case of *Bazley v Curry*:

> a focus on policy is not to diminish the importance of legal principle … However, in areas of jurisprudence where changes have been occurring in response to policy considerations, the best route to enduring principle may well lie through policy.[51]

On the other hand, it acknowledges Lord Hobhouse's criticism of McLachlin's 'social and economic reasons' in *Lister*, where Hobhouse made it clear that 'the exposition of the policy reasons for a rule is not the same as defining the criteria for its application'.[52] Weighing up both approaches Ward undeniably acknowledges that policy considerations do and should inform legal principles provided they are 'developed incrementally and in a principled way'.[53] This chimes with feminist perspectives on the need to adopt a more modern and sensitive approach to vicarious liability. The policy dimension has been well expressed in the UK Supreme Court by Lord Phillips.[54] The 'defined edge' comes with Phillips's observation that:

> the policy objective underlying vicarious liability is to ensure, insofar as it is fair, just and reasonable, that liability for tortious wrong is borne by a defendant with the means to compensate the victim.[55]

The moral balance influencing the Supreme Court's conclusions in the Birmingham Archdiocesan appeal in the *Maga* case references the largest claim against the Roman Catholic Church, made by Patrick Raggett.[56] A city lawyer, he had been regularly abused over a four-year period by a teacher at the Jesuit Catholic College he had attended in the 1970s. Raggett sought £5 million in compensation after suffering a breakdown in 2005 and suddenly remembering that Father Michael Spencer had abused him, touching his genitals and performing digital anal penetration. Spencer had died in 2000, aged 76, but Raggett sued the Governors of the College, who denied liability on the basis that the claim was time-barred as it had not been brought within three years of Raggett's eighteenth birthday as per section 11 *Limitation Act 1980*. However, in the High Court, Mrs Justice Swift directed that the section 11 bar should not apply, being satisfied with Raggett's claim of suppressed memory accounting for the delay.[57] She followed the 2008 House of Lords decision

[49] At paras 52–54.

[50] Cited in Giliker Paula *Vicarious Liability in Tort: A Comparative Perspective* Cambridge University Press Cambridge 2010 p 244.

[51] *Bazeley v Curry* [1999] 2 SCR 534.

[52] *Lister v Hesley Hall* [2002] 1 AC 215; [2001] UKHL 22 para 60.

[53] *JGE v The Trustees of the Portsmouth Roman Catholic Diocesan Trust* [2013] QB 722; [2012] EWCA Civ 938.

[54] *The Catholic Welfare Society v Various Claimants* [2013] 2 AC 1; [2012] UKSC 56.

[55] At para 34.

[56] *Raggett v Society of Jesus Trust for Roman Catholic Purposes* [2009] EWHC 909 (QB).

[57] As above.

in *A v Hoare*, a set of conjoined appeals.[58] The House of Lords held that for compensation claims for personal injury in cases of historic sexual abuse, time ran (under section 14 of the Act) from when the claimant had knowledge of the necessary facts of any abuse, not from when he or she could have been expected to take certain steps to report the original abuse.[59]

While Mrs Justice Swift agreed that not all the problems of Raggett's adult life were a consequence of the abuse, she emphasised that as 'the victim of an insidious form of abuse involving a grave breach of trust' he had 'suffered significantly' and in so doing, provided his claim with a level of validation in line with that which he was seeking, as his own comments make plain.[60] Raggett was scathing of the Church's responses and the ongoing breach of trust that represented for him:

> The most important aspect of this trial is that the people who allowed this to happen — and who were quite happy to see it swept under the carpet — have been held responsible at last … For all the warm words from the Jesuit order about co-operating in this case, the reality is they fought it tooth and nail without regard for my feelings … the Catholic Church generally, is still not accepting legal and moral responsibility for the dark virus of abuse in the way it should.[61]

This once again returns the focus to the feminist critiques of vicarious liability as traditionally conceived, and the argument that for the law to work effectively, it must work in a social context that acknowledges the need for changes in how institutions perceive their responsibility for offenders as well as for victims.

6.0 'Equality-Before-the-Law' and Religious Institutions

Bender insists that:

> Accompanying our ideology of equality-before-the-law is an expectation that the judge and legal process somehow will intervene, if necessary, to balance the unequal power between the parties, so that justice can prevail.[62]

Such power dynamics can and should not simply be ignored or dismissed because the autonomy of the law privileges more objective and universal principles. There has been discernible movement. Claims for intentional sexual assault (trespass against the person) once fell within the breach of duty category,[63] but in *Stubbings v Webb*[64]

[58] *A v Hoare* [2008] 1 AC 844.

[59] An interesting viewpoint on the limitation issue in a Canadian context can be found in Adjin-Tettey Elizabeth and Koddar Freya 'Improving the Potential of Tort Law for Redressing Historical Abuse Claims: The Need for a Contextualized Approach to the Limitation Defence' (2010–11) 42 *Ottawa Law Review* 95.

[60] *Raggett v Preston Catholic College Governors* [2012] EWHC 3641 (QB); 'Jesuit-Run College Abuse Victim Patrick Raggett Wins Damages' *BBC News* 9 November 2012 <http://www.bbc.co.uk/news/uk-england-london-20267571> Accessed 23 February 2015.

[61] Gledhill Ruth 'Lawyer Can Sue Jesuits for £5m Over Abuse' *The Times* 6 May 2009.

[62] Bender 'Feminist (Re)torts' above note 8 at 884.

[63] Long established in *Letang v Cooper* [1965] 1 QB 232; *Long v Hepworth* [1968] 1 WLR 1299.

[64] *Stubbings v Webb* [1993] AC 498.

(concerning a claim of sexual abuse committed over 20 years before) the House of Lords ruled that such cases were now excluded from sections 11, 14 and 33 of the *Limitation Act 1980* which, in combination, had previously permitted such claims. Burton confirms that *Stubbings* 'produced severe distortions in the lower courts who attempted to distinguish it on grounds which created both anomalies and complexity'.[65] Claimants of historic abuse were now required to prove that defendant organisations had been 'systematically negligent' in failing to respond to and deal with any allegations. Practically speaking, the legal discourse was clearly discriminating against those with an inherent 'historic disadvantage' as well as condoning the power imbalance between the parties. But in overruling *Stubbings*, Lord Hoffman in *Hoare* delivered the lead opinion criticising the panel for deciding the case 'as if the 1954 Act had just been passed' and pointing out that, by way of a model, the High Court of Australia had declined to follow it.[66]

Hoffman dismissed the 'systematically negligent' requirement suggesting that future claimants should instead rely on vicarious liability.[67] Other aspects corrected in his reasoning would appear to be in line with feminist scholarship. However, feminist responses would be dissatisfied with the continuing limitations on the interpretation of what constitutes 'significant injury'. Thus under section 14(2) of the *Limitation Act* in the context of child sexual abuse: 'an injury is significant' only if 'the person whose date of knowledge is in question would reasonably have considered it sufficiently serious to justify his instituting proceedings'. Yet young children may not realise that their abuse is 'sufficiently serious'; they are also unlikely to appreciate the need to, and implications of, 'instituting proceedings'. While the provision allows both actual knowledge 'observed by' the claimant and constructive knowledge such as medical and paediatric expertise to be taken into account, the section remains vague as to whether individual characteristics caused by the abusive behaviour could be considered. Moreover, the judiciary over-complicated the test of whether a reasonable person with that knowledge would consider the injury sufficiently serious making it partly objective and partly subjective.[68]

Bender's position on the 'injured parties' would be clear: that they are not only 'burdened by the pain, injustice, and disruptions caused by their injuries, but they also are tangled in a legal system which is unfamiliar, alienating and ritualised'.[69] Therefore what constitutes 'reasonableness' needs to be more generously and flexibly interpreted, paralleling Hoffman's conclusion that a claimant's injuries would be established as a 'significant injury' where he was 'obviously aware that he had been seriously assaulted', either at the time or realised such years later.[70] Lady Hale admitted that she found the provision more difficult to construe but 'despite my

[65] Burton Frank 'Limitation, Vicarious Liability and Historic Actions for Abuse: A Changing Legal Landscape' (2013) *Journal of Personal Injury Law* 95.
[66] *A v Hoare* [2008] 1 AC 844 [2008] UKHL 6 para 17; para 20; *Stringel v Clark* (2006) 226 CLR 442 considering *Kruber v Grzesiak* [1963] VR 621.
[67] As above.
[68] At para 34 et seq.
[69] Bender 'Feminist (Re)torts' above note 8 at 883.
[70] *A v Hoare* [2008] 1 AC 844 [2008] UKHL 6 paras 40–43. Despite subsequent conflicting expert opinion casting doubt on whether he 'really' knew.

nagging doubts' fully supported Lord Hoffman's 'more generous approach to the exercise of discretion'.[71] Lord Brown acknowledged their Lordships were 'ushering in' a 'new era' and with it the likelihood of more sexual abuse claims.[72] The ruling was followed in *Raggett* and *B v Nugent Care Society* concerning three test cases in respect of a group litigation comprising 60 claimants who had been sexually abused in the 1960s and 1970s at two residential Catholic schools.[73] The Court of Appeal in *Nugent* issued guidance on the correct approach in applying section 33 of the *Limitation Act* post-*Hoare*. First, the claimant need only show that the alleged abuse occurred and caused the alleged psychological or physical damage and that the defendant was vicariously liable for it. Second, the question of whether the claimant could reasonably have been expected to institute proceedings is to be determined by the judge under section 33, whereas pre-*Hoare* it had only been treated as relevant to the claimant's knowledge and not to the exercise of the discretion.

These discussions on the moral responsibility of Roman Catholic parish priests and teachers for their congregations and pupils, and the legal responsibility of their parent (employing) Church, have been rehearsed at length. This is because they represent the extent to which the Roman Catholic Church in the UK has been forced by the courts into accepting its legal responsibility for the actions of its 'employees'. The decision in *The Catholic Child Welfare Society*[74] case has gone a considerable way towards reflecting a measure of divergence from a traditionally rigid doctrine on vicarious liability in relation to the Roman Catholic Church. To date, it has only been the Roman Catholic Church which has been required to take responsibility via the doctrines of vicarious liability, for the tortious actions of their clergy and associated agents.

7.0 Responsibility and Religious Institutions

In relation to 'responsibility' Bender makes a clear distinction between corporate and individual liability. Corporate liability should relate to the harms caused vicariously whereas personal responsibility must 'correlate with the power of individuals' and their authority to 'make decisions about resources, markets, personnel, and safety, as well as power to disclose'.[75] The Roman Catholic Church has significant power and authoritative responsibility to make decisions about its personnel and the safety of those under their care and it is on these grounds that courts have agreed that it must be held accountable. However, there can be no assumption that, in England, the Anglican Church is equally vulnerable. It might be thought unlikely, following Lord Phillips's exposition of policy, that the quirks of theology and the arcane complexity of the Anglican Church's legal position will continue to challenge the ability of the courts to establish vicarious liability against the institution in England should a claim be brought against it. Yet even in the post-*Catholic Child Welfare* environment

[71] At paras 56–59.
[72] At para 84.
[73] *B v Nugent Care Society* [2009] EWCA Civ 827.
[74] *Catholic Child Welfare Society v Various claimants* [2013] 2 AC 1; [2012] UKSC 56.
[75] Bender 'Feminist (Re)torts' above note 8 at 870.

in England, it is likely to be more than just a matter of time before or if the current apparent impunity of that Church changes. A recent judgment has suggested that it remains difficult to establish a traditional employment relationship for Protestant churches generally.[76]

Despite its position as the Established Church, the Church of England is not a single legal entity. Equally, Anglican parochial clergy are not employees, but office holders and the right of appointment to an office does not automatically lie with the Church hierarchy and often still lies with the (secular) patron of an individual living. Their rights and duties as office holders are regulated not by an employment contract but by the laws relating to the office held: independent of the individual holding it.[77] As clarified in *Sharpe v Worcester Diocesan Board of Finance & Another* the position of a rector in relation to his diocese or the over-arching body of the Church of England is, under ecclesiastical law, very distinctly not that of an employee.[78] The Church can and does issue guidance to incumbents on how to perform the duties of their office satisfactorily according to current expectations, but even the Bishop's Papers cannot be held to amount to any form of employment contract as it is within the rights of Anglican clergy to decline to follow the advice on policy expressed in them.[79]

The position in ecclesiastical and employment law is that where a senior cleric has power over an individual cleric, it relates only to their spiritual authority as clerics. Using that spiritual authority, under ecclesiastical law, a cleric may be defrocked for conduct unbecoming to a cleric in holy orders. That sanction has been rarely used. Instead, the Anglican Church in England has preferred to resort to removing an individual's licence to officiate and preach at any service outside their own parish, either permanently or for a period of years.[80] The Church has very recently shown itself reluctant to apply that remedy to its clergy even after conviction on charges of sexual abuse. Most recently, a furore has arisen over Reverend Guy Bennett, formerly Rector of Oxted and Tandridge, convicted in 1999 on charges of indecent assault against young girls.[81] He was, that year, deprived of his licence to hold office in the Church, but has not been defrocked. In October 2014, the Archbishop of Canterbury wrote to one of Bennett's victims, outraged that he was attending church in East Grinstead, Sussex, regretting that it was not possible to stop anyone from wearing a dog-collar or using the honorific Reverend, so long as

[76] *President of the Methodist Conference v Preston* [2013] 2 AC 163.

[77] See *Ecclesiastical Offices (Terms of Service) Regulations 2009* (UK) Regulation 33, which applies Part X of the *Employment Rights Act 1996* (UK) *as if*, and not *because*, clergy are employed. Since 2011, most Anglican clerics hold their offices under Common Tenure.

[78] *Sharpe v Worcester Diocesan Board of Finance* [2012] ET 1302291/2008 and 1316848/2009, upheld by the Court of Appeal in *Sharpe v Bishop of Worcester* [2015] EWCA Civ 399.

[79] Church of England DDO Handbook, which is only available online at <https://www.churchofengland.org/clergy-office-holders/ministry/selection/ddos/ddo-handbook.aspx> Accessed 14 September 2015.

[80] See the decision to remove the licence of Reverend Patrick Okechi for a period of 10 years where an adulterous affair with a parishioner was held to constitute a breach of trust <http://www.ecclaw.co.uk/clergydiscipline/okechi2.pdf> Accessed 14 September 2015.

[81] 'Vicar Faces Jail Over Indecent Assault' *BBC News* 30 April 1999 <http://news.bbc.co.uk/1/hi/uk/332679.stm> Accessed 13 July 2015.

there was no illegal purpose in so doing. He added that having taken advice, it was also his conclusion that he 'did not have the powers to depose Bennett from clerical orders'.[82]

There is also the complication of the issue of the unique financial position of the Church of England as the State Church in England. As office holders, clergy are in receipt of stipends provided by the Central Stipends Authority, run by the Church Commissioners. The Church Commissioners were established by Parliament through the Church Commissioners Measure 1947, as an independent secular statutory body with responsibility for managing the Church's assets and finances.[83] The objective was to ensure that the Church would not become a burden on taxpayers, but in practice, the senior ecclesiastical hierarchy of the Church does not have the power to manage its finances without the agreement of the Church Commissioners, as attempts to persuade the Commissioners to invest 'ethically' underline.[84]

Such legal ambiguities surrounding the position of the Anglican Church in England perhaps help to explain why the conviction (along with his organist) in April 2013 of Reverend Keith Wilkie Denford, formerly parish priest at St John the Evangelist, Burgess Hill, on three charges of indecent assaults on boys under 16 has not been followed up by any broader claim against the Church of England. Instead, public reportage of the case has sought to emphasise that the Diocese of Chichester had taken pains to act properly and promptly once it learned officially of the abuse.[85] In response to media questioning about the diocesan response, the Bishop, Martin Warner, has pointed out that reportage of the abuse by one of the victims had only been made in 2011. At that point the Diocese had been swift to involve the police and to aid them in developing the case for prosecution.[86]

Even in the Anglican Church of Australia, where the position of clerics is less complicated by such arcane laws dating back to the time of the English Church's establishment in the sixteenth century, there have not yet been successful claims against it for vicarious liability in sexual abuse cases.[87] But it has at least shown itself willing to act (if as discreetly as possible) to defrock those found guilty of the sexual abuse of children. As a result of amendments to its canon law, Church Discipline Ordinance 2006, and the Holy Orders, Relinquishment and Deposition Canon 2004, it is even reported to be planning to laicise a former Bishop, Keith Slater, for failing to take action on incidents of abuse by clergy within his diocese.[88] This may provide a

[82] The letter has been published on a number of websites: <https://theneedleblog.wordpress.com/2014/12/13/archbishop-of-canterbury-tells-survivor-that-paedophile-vicar-will-not-be-defrocked/> Accessed 14 September 2015.

[83] *Church Commissioners Measure* (1947) (UK).

[84] See *Harries v Church Commissioners for England* [1992] 1 WLR 1241.

[85] 'Child Abuse Pair Found Guilty' *Church Times* 12 April 2013 <http://www.churchtimes.co.uk/articles/2013/12-april/news/uk/child-abuse-pair-found-guilty> Accessed 13 July 2015.

[86] As above.

[87] As noted above there has also been a difficulty with vicarious liability claims relating to the Roman Catholic Church in Australia.

[88] *Church Discipline Ordinance 2006* (NSW); *Holy Orders, Relinquishment and Deposition Canon 2004* (UK). See <http://www.abc.net.au/news/2015-03-18/former-bishop-keith-slater-to-face-defrocking-by-anglican-church/6328112> Accessed 14 September 2015.

model which the Anglican Church in England might be wise to follow, in terms of maintaining a genuine spiritual authority rooted in a popular conviction that the Church takes seriously its moral duties of care, even though as at the time of writing there are still no instances of successful vicarious liability claims.

8.0 Compensation

The practice of compensating in monetary terms for damage and hurt done according to a sliding financial scale is long-established.[89] The *Catholic Child Welfare* judgment certainly reflects that, in line with Lord Phillips's policy reasoning, 'the employer, by employing the employee to carry on the activity will have created the risk of the tort committed by the employee',[90] as reaffirming that direction. While there are times when purely financial compensation is important, modern appreciations of the value of the individual and the importance placed on emotionally sensitive responses by the courts are likely to make it more difficult for those seeking compensation to accept it *solely* in the form of a financial restitution.

While victims, such as those discussed previously in this article, have expressed a desire for apologies, some distrust remains about the genuineness of those offered by the Christian churches. What alternative reparation might be acceptable, either instead of or accompanying financial compensation? Bender suggests a way forward would be for common law tort theory 'to acknowledge that financial responsibility alone is inadequate for legal responsibility' and that instead it must 'imagine another medium of value' which amounts to a 'recognition that injury is an emotional, physical, and spiritual event'.[91] She asserts that a feminist voice of responsibility, which includes emotional, caregiving work, has not been readily translatable into money, so tort law has basically ignored it. She further advocates a reappraisal of the conceptualisation of injury to include recognition that injury is an emotional, physical and spiritual event.[92]

The importance of an apology accompanying a successful vicarious liability claim against the Roman Catholic Church has already been mentioned, as has been the willingness of the Church of England to apologise, at least broadly and generically, for sexual abuse by Anglican clergy in the UK.[93] Yet as Nick Smith has pointed out, the issue of remorse for crimes and wrongdoing, and apologies ordered by law, sets up a series of complex issues, at least partly because so much of the moral origins of English law lie within canon and ecclesiastical law.[94] An expectation of the expression of contrition for individual wrongdoing is a core element in the

[89] Brundage James *Law, Sex and Christian Society in Medieval Europe* University of Chicago Chicago 1987.

[90] *Catholic Child Welfare Society v Various claimants* [2013] 2 AC 1; [2012] UKSC 56 para 35.

[91] Bender 'Feminist (Re)torts' above note 8 at 905.

[92] As above.

[93] Graham Georgie and Bingham John 'Justin Welby: I Broke Down in Tears at Horror of Church Child Abuse' *Daily Telegraph* 27 October 2014 <http://www.telegraph.co.uk/news/religion/11190890/Justin-Welby-I-broke-down-in-tears-at-horror-of-Church-child-abuse.html> Accessed 23 February 2015.

[94] Smith above note 7; also Helmholtz Richard and Baker John *Oxford History of the Laws of England* Oxford University Press Oxford 2004.

rituals of the Christian churches, as the General Confession in the Book of Common Prayer has underlined for Anglicans who are required to state publicly that they had 'offended against thy holy laws' by having (amongst other things) 'done those things which we ought not to have done'.[95] To gain absolution from sins, genuine remorse was required, largely testified to by the public nature of the confession of sins.

Given this background, the force of apologies from the Church of England, expressed by its senior clerics, does have value. As well as echoing restorative justice thinking about the need for public justice to involve harm vindication, it is also in line with Bender and Honore's requirement that redress should, to amount to justice, involve an acknowledgement and affirmation of the fact of individual suffering as a result of child sexual abuse in order to provide the necessary 'sensitivity to the experiences of the parties'.[96] A change to Church ordinances to permit an easier laicisation of clerical abusers could, in practice, be the most practical way forward for the Church of England to show at least a moral, if not a legal, appreciation of a vicarious liability for its vicars.

9.0 Conclusion

This discussion has demonstrated that, in the wake of the high-profile clerical abuse cases discussed here, the English courts are responding positively to the challenges posed by feminist scholarship. In line with that scholarship, what the legal thinking surrounding the issue of vicarious liability has begun to show is a recognition that, because the matter involves a breach of trust by men with a duty of care for the souls, rather than simply the bodies, of victims, financial compensation has not been seen as sufficient recompense by many claimants. In expanding its thinking to reflect some of the approaches intrinsic to restorative justice, the law is recognising the importance of the wider social and institutional context in its decisions. This has, most recently, been shown in the High Court decision in the case of *A v Watchtower Bible and Tract Society*, where the Society was held vicariously liable in a case of child sexual abuse.[97] Though not strictly constituted a Christian Church analogous to the Methodist, Baptist, Presbyterian and Unitarian Churches, the Society does make claims to a similar moral status, making the decision relevant here.

The ability for the civil law to provide a remedy, albeit imperfectly if seen solely in terms of financial redress, is capable of producing accountability at a higher level. If tortious liability is about corrective justice, and a component of that correction is rooted in an enterprise-risk policy imperative, it is not difficult to see how an organised Church is now subject to greater and more transparent risk management obligations. However, it is not necessarily the case that the Church of England would so qualify, something underlined by the ongoing omission by Synod in July 2015 of any suggestion of planning for financial compensation to be paid by the Church in clergy abuse cases.[98] Given this, what alternative reparation can be appropriate? The Church of

[95] General Confession *Book of Common Prayer*, Church of England 1662.
[96] Bender 'Feminist (Re)torts' above note 8 at 876; Honore above note 28.
[97] *A v Trustees of the Watchtower Bible and Tract Society* [2015] EWHC 1722 (QB).
[98] 'Sunday' *BBC Radio 4* 12 July 2015.

England has only accepted a moral liability for abuse perpetrated by clergy belonging to them. Beyond that, for reasons to do with its complex and arcane legal position, the Church as an institution has not yet received an equivalent scrutiny by the courts in relation to vicarious liability. The potential for a challenge to its impunity remains, not only through revelations by the Goddard enquiry[99] into child abuse by UK institutions which will include the Church of England, but more immediately with the forthcoming trial (currently scheduled for October 2015) of the retired Bishop of Gloucester. Peter Ball is charged both with child sexual abuse and misconduct in public office, possible because of his Episcopal role which places him in a different position to parish clergy.[100] Though he may, in the end, be found unfit to plead, it is likely that, echoing the decision in the Lord Janner case, a decision will be made to proceed with a hearing of facts at least on the abuse charges.

[99] Independent Inquiry into Child Sexual Abuse (England and Wales). The enquiry started 9 July 2015 and is expected to last up to 2020 <https://www.csa-inquiry.independent.gov.uk/> Accessed 14 September 2015.

[100] 'Judge to Decide Whether Bishop Accused of Sex Assault Crimes Will Stand Trial' *The Guardian* 1 May 2015 <http://www.theguardian.com/uk-news/2015/may/01/judge-to-decide-whether-bishop-accused-of-sex-assault-crimes-will-stand-trial> Accessed 13 July 2015.

An Unexpected Path: Bankruptcy, Justice and Intersecting Identities in the Catholic Sexual Abuse Scandals

Meredith Edelman

Abstract. This article will discuss how various identities inhabited by victims of child sexual abuse by Catholic clergy may impact survivors' ability to find justice through legal processes. It also highlights two examples of patterns of response to allegations of sexual abuse by clergy in the United States. In prominent urban archdioceses, empowered survivors, often members of dominant social groups, have successfully utilised media and legal process — resulting in criminal convictions, large awards in civil court and the implementation of new prevention efforts. In large part, the public perception of who survivors are is based on this model. This article will discuss how this perception may be inaccurate; survivors in subaltern communities are likely to be under-represented, not only in public perception but also in terms of access to legal process and remedies. In certain US jurisdictions, however, bankruptcy cases filed by Catholic organisations may prove to be an intriguing legal process whereby some survivors have been able to secure remedies that could be described as restorative. Two of these jurisdictions, where most survivors are indigenous or Hispanic, will be highlighted in this article in order to consider how mechanisms other than traditional civil litigation may lower barriers to legal remedies.

1.0 Introduction

Kimberle Crenshaw wrote in 1991:

> [w]here systems of race, gender, and class domination converge, as they do in the experiences of battered women of colour, intervention strategies based solely in the experiences of women who do not share the same class or race backgrounds will be of limited help to women who because of race and class face different obstacles.[1]

My objective in this article is to consider differences in terms of access to justice through legal process along lines of race, gender, class domination and childhood

---

[1] Crenshaw Kimberle 'Mapping the Margins: Intersectionality, Identity Politics, and Violence Against Women of Color' (1991) 43 *Stanford Law Review* 1241 at 1246.

vulnerability. I hope to contribute to understandings of how cultural conceptions of abuse and those affected by it may render some victims invisible. They might also be less likely to have their claims adjudicated, or if they do seek justice, receive less in compensation. I briefly trace a history of the sexual abuse scandal affecting the Catholic Archdiocese in Boston, Massachusetts and compare it to how the scandal has unfolded in two rural, economically disadvantaged areas — northern Alaska and northern New Mexico and Arizona. I hope that the examination of how scandal progressed in the urban and rural jurisdictions might help illuminate how different types of legal mechanisms may affect the likelihood that survivors access justice through the legal system.

Sexual abuse of children by Catholic clergy, and the problems of subsequent cover-ups, denials and failures of leaders to respond appropriately are documented in Austria, Australia, Belgium, Canada, Chile, France, Germany, Ireland, Italy, Kenya, Malta, Mexico, the Netherlands, the Philippines, Poland, the United States and elsewhere.[2] Legal systems have approached this problem in different ways in various places. There have been criminal prosecutions of abusers as well as of leaders and even dioceses failing to report abuse to civil authorities or actively concealing evidence.[3] Individuals have brought civil claims. Royal Commissions and other formal investigations and reports have brought evidence and truth to light. In the United States, civil litigation has cost Catholic organisations well over $3 billion.[4] Some dioceses and religious orders have filed for bankruptcy protection. This article is intended to explore how different mechanisms affect the kinds of justice that survivors obtain through legal process.

There is good reason to believe that the scandal has unfolded in different ways along intersections of identity. Although white men are prominently featured by survivors' advocacy groups and media portrayals of clerical abuse survivors, there is little data available to show the rates of victimisation among different groups of people. Further, there are good reasons to believe that, at least in the United States and perhaps Australia, indigenous, African American, Hispanic and immigrant communities are over-represented as victims.[5] It is hoped that a discussion of select examples of responses to clerical sexual abuse may add to an understanding of how intersecting identities and different mechanisms can affect access to legal remedies. The purpose of this article is not to speak for survivors of sexual abuse,[6] but rather to pay close

---

[2] Center for Constitutional Rights on behalf of the Survivors Network of those Abused by Priests *Shadow Report Prepared for 52nd Session of the UN Committee Against Torture in Connection with its Review of the Holy See* (2014) p 6.

[3] *Minnesota v Archdiocese of Saint Paul and Minneapolis*, Ramsey County District Court No. 2139124–1 (2015); Collins Jon and Baran Madeleine 'Twin Cities Archdiocese Criminally Charged in Priest Child Abuse Case' *MPR News* (online) 5 June 2015 <http://www.mprnews.org/story/2015/06/05/archdiocese-investigation> Accessed 26 August 2015.

[4] 'The Catholic Church in America: Earthly Concerns' *The Economist* 18 August 2012 (online) <http://www.economist.com/node/21560536> Accessed 26 August 2015.

[5] Advocacy and support organisations use the term 'survivors' with reference to those who experienced abuse, in large part to emphasise the humanity and agency of those people. That term will be used for the purposes of this article.

[6] Howe Adrian 'Addressing Child Sexual Assault in Australian Aboriginal Communities: The Politics of White Voice' (2009) 30 *Australian Feminist Law Journal* 41.

attention to how the scandal developed in different ways along intersecting lines of identity in the United States as well as question the dominant cultural understanding of who survivors are.

2.0 Patterns of Response

This section describes how the scandal unfolded in Boston, and compares one of the dioceses in the United States which has drawn significant media and academic attention, with areas in northern Alaska, Arizona and New Mexico (the 'Rural Dioceses'), which have attracted far less attention to date from major media sources.

2.1 *Archdiocese of Boston*

In Boston, the scandal of clerical sexual abuse of children has been very much in the public consciousness. Settlements and legal cases cost the Archdiocese of Boston hundreds of millions of dollars, yet many despair of ever feeling that justice has been served — as the payouts and publicity seem to have little effect on the Archdiocese's power and resources. Laws and policies are changed but concerns about compliance and consistency remain. There are even concerns about the efficacy of efforts to prevent future abuse, one of the reasons many survivors point to as a motivating factor in coming forward.

In early 2002, after many years during which a survivor advocacy movement had little traction among the general public, stories of abuse, cover-ups and poor treatment of survivors were brought to the forefront through a series of articles in the *Boston Globe.* The *Boston Globe* investigation into the litigation and allegations regarding one particular priest — John Geoghan — and the Archdiocese of Boston's covering up the allegations while he had continued access to children was in many ways a spark that incited widespread discussion and public awareness of the issue internationally.[7] Within two years, the Cardinal had resigned, 150 priests in Boston had been accused of sexual abuse and more than 500 survivors had filed claims.[8]

An investigation conducted by the Massachusetts Attorney General's office found that Cardinal Bernard Law and his predecessors in office had routinely sought to protect abusive clergy and Church reputation instead of considering the needs of children and victims, despite knowing about the abuse.[9] Massachusetts introduced laws requiring clergy to report any knowledge of abuse to the civil authorities. Many clergy were tried and convicted under criminal laws, including Geoghan.

---

[7] Henley Jon 'How the *Boston Globe* Exposed the Abuse Scandal that Rocked the Catholic Church' *The Guardian* (online) 22 April 2010 < http://www.theguardian.com/world/2010/apr/21/boston-globe-abuse-scandal-catholic> Accessed 26 August 2015.

[8] As above.

[9] Office of the Attorney General of the Commonwealth of Massachusetts *The Sexual Abuse of Children in the Roman Catholic Archdiocese of Boston* 2003 p 25–30.

The United States Conference of Catholic Bishops (the 'USCCB') drew up a charter for the protection of children. In March 2002, the Archdiocese agreed to a $30 million settlement with 86 survivors who had been abused by Geoghan.[10] In 2003, the Archdiocese agreed to an $85 million settlement with more than 550 other survivors.[11] The Boston Archdiocese began releasing financial records, detailing in its June 2005 report that it paid more than $127 million to survivors.[12] The most recent financial report published by the Archdiocese shows that during the years 2013–14, the Archdiocese paid over $3.25 million to 49 survivors, with $5 million reserved to pay future claims. The organisation has exhausted funds available from insurers.[13]

An audit commissioned by the USCCB found that, in Boston, as well as every diocese audited:

> individuals coming forward with allegations are treated with respect and offered assistance in their healing process. Those making allegations are not required to sign confidentiality agreements. Reports of child sexual abuse are reported to civil authorities and priests who were found to have committed sexual abuse of minors are removed from ministry. Dioceses … are being open and transparent with the faithful, informing communities affected by abuse. Adults who work around children are being trained to create safe environments and to be attentive to the behavior of others; this includes clergy, employees, and volunteers — even children are being taught to be aware of signs of grooming and to report it. Clergy, employees, and volunteers undergo background evaluations; dioceses/eparchies have instituted rigorous screening and evaluation processes for men seeking to enter the seminary and the priesthood. Clergy with credible allegations are not transferred to other parishes or dioceses/eparchies, and there are on-going, regular conversations between major superiors and bishops about the religious men assigned to a diocese/eparchy.[14]

Although the results of this audit sound encouraging, a closer look shows its almost complete dependence on information provided by dioceses and religious orders.[15] The data provided was frequently inconsistent or incomplete, was inconsistently collected and some dioceses refused to participate at all.[16] This and other USCCB-

[10] Jones Richard Lezin 'Former Altar Boy Describes Years of Abuse, Then Years of Silence' *New York Times* 18 March 2002 (online) <http://www.nytimes.com/2002/03/18/nyregion/former-altar-boy-describes-years-of-abuse-then-years-of-silence.html?pagewanted=2> Accessed 26 August 2015.

[11] Associate Press 'Boston Archdiocese Agrees to $85M Sex Abuse Settlement' 9 September 2003 (online) <http://www.foxnews.com/story/2003/09/09/boston-archdiocese-agrees-to-85m-sex-abuse-settlement/> Accessed 26 August 2015.

[12] Archdiocese of Boston *Source and Use of Funds: Financial Disclosure of the Archdiocese of Boston Regarding Sexual Abuse Settlements and Related Costs* 19 April 2006 (online) <http://www.bostoncatholic.org/Offices-And-Services/Office-Detail.aspx?id=14190&pid=508> Accessed 26 August 2015.

[13] Archdiocese of Boston *2014 Financial Report* (online) <http://www.bostoncatholic.org/uploadedFiles/BostonCatholicorg/Offices_And_Services/Offices/Sub_Pages/Finance_and_Technology/FY14/AnnualReportFY14Final.pdf> Accessed 26 August 2015.

[14] Secretariat of Child and Youth Protection *2014 Annual Report: Findings and Recommendations* March 2015 (online) <http://www.usccb.org/issues-and-action/child-and-youth-protection/upload/2014-Annual-Report.pdf> Accessed 26 August 2015.

[15] As above.

[16] As above.

commissioned audits have been described by survivor advocates as 'nearly meaningless'. Advocates for survivors assert that the Church is not capable of policing itself and that 'the crime of church higher-ups hiding and transferring offending priests is a persistent problem'.[17]

The audits and policy changes are called insufficient given suspicions that children are still at risk of abuse by clergy. A 2011 report from a Philadelphia grand jury — a city not far from Boston and which had similarly been found in compliance by the audit — highlights these suspicions. By 2011, two previous grand juries in Philadelphia had already issued reports detailing continued abuse and cover-ups by officials within the Archdiocese in Philadelphia. The 2011 Grand Jury reported that:

> [t]he rapist priests we accuse were well known to the Secretary of Clergy, but he cloaked their conduct and put them in place to do it again. The procedures implemented by the Archdiocese to help victims are in fact designed to help the abusers, and the Archdiocese itself. Worst of all, apparent abusers — dozens of them, we believe — remain on duty in the Archdiocese, today, with open access to new young prey.[18]

These reports lead people to wonder whether 'a diocese [might] provide all the necessary safe-environment programs and screenings and still fail to protect the welfare of minors?'.[19]

Further, although litigation has resulted in large awards, Balboni observed that many survivors bringing claims in Boston found the process traumatic.[20] Survivors were looking for 'public acknowledgement of their pain, acceptance of responsibility for wrongdoing by the Church, and opportunity for voice (representativeness), and an apology'.[21] She concluded that the need for an acknowledgement of abuse was generally met in that survivors told their stories, were believed and created a supportive environment among themselves.[22]

The adversarial process incentivises defendants not to admit any fault. This means that survivors bringing claims have to prove the truth of their abuse — which means they required records held by the Archdiocese. Plaintiffs had to tell their stories to their own lawyers, in depositions, often in settlement negotiations, at trial. These statements are made with the knowledge that judges, jurors, attorneys, Church officials and members of the public will hear and read about what happened to them. Obtaining records from the Church through discovery can be frustrating. Even where claims are brought by survivors as a group, easing some of the trauma of litigation, Balboni found that reaching a settlement did not put the pain to an end. Many Boston settlement agreements allowed the Archdiocese not to admit any liability for

[17] Stern Andrew 'Catholic Church Says Child Abuse Cases Rose in 2011' *Reuters US Edition* 10 April 2012 (online) <http://www.reuters.com/article/2012/04/10/us-usa-catholic-abuse-idUSBRE8391HF20120410> Accessed 26 August 2015.

[18] *In re County Investigating: Grand Jury XXIII* Misc No. 0009901–2008.

[19] Frawley Desmond Joan 'Philadelphia and the Dallas Charter' *National Catholic Register* (2011) (online) <http://www.ncregister.com/daily-news/philadelphia-and-the-dallas-charter/> Accessed 26 August 2015.

[20] Balboni Jennifer M *Clergy Sexual Abuse Litigation: Survivors Seeking Justice* First Forum Press Boulder 2011 p 125.

[21] As above at 133.

[22] As above at 72, 126.

abuse.[23] She found that arbitration pitted survivors against each other in a 'zero sum game' to determine recoveries, and that the incentive of higher payments for more pain and suffering caused anguish for many.[24]

2.2 *Rural Dioceses*

In poorer, more rural areas of the US — perhaps especially those with high proportions of minority groups — distinctions emerge in the model of response. In the western states of America, parishioners are more likely to be Hispanic — about one third of Catholics in the US are Hispanic — many living in the south western US.[25] As discussed above, there is no empirical research comparing the rates of victimisation by Catholic clergy among people of different racial and ethnic groups. However, the sheer number of people coming forward to report abuse occurring in the parishes, missions and boarding schools first established for the conversion or assimilation of indigenous people is staggering. Survivors filed lawsuits claiming that '[n]ative villages in the state of Alaska were essentially a dumping ground for Jesuit priests unsuited to serve anywhere else in the Jesuit organization'.[26] In one investigation, it was found that 80% of the children in a particular village were sexually abused.[27] The Jesuits in the Northwest, which operated missions and boarding schools in Washington, Oregon and Alaska, settled the claims of at least 635 people in 2007 and 2011, almost all of them Native American, who had been abused at these missions and schools.[28]

The Rural Dioceses are two of the poorest dioceses in the United States. In Fairbanks, '[o]nly eight (8) of its forty-six (46) parishes and missions are self-supporting. Many of the parishioners … live the subsistence lifestyle (subsisting on hunting, fishing and gathering)'.[29] Bishop Wall of the Diocese of Gallup calls it the poorest diocese in the United States. He notes the high proportions of Native American and Hispanic people in the small diocese, as well as the high rates of poverty.[30]

---

[23] As above at 134.
[24] As above at 125.
[25] Funk Cary and Martínez Jessica 'Fewer Hispanics are Catholic, so How Can More Catholics be Hispanic?' *Factank: News in the Numbers* 7 May 2014 (online) <http://www.pewresearch.org/fact-tank/2014/05/07/fewer-hispanics-are-catholic-so-how-can-more-catholics-be-hispanic/> Accessed 26 August 2015.
[26] Associated Press 'Jesuit Priests Accused of Sex Abuse in Alaska' *Seattle Post-Intelligencer* 14 January 2009 (online) <http://www.bishop-accountability.org/news2009/01_02/2009_01_14_AP_JesuitPriests.htm> Accessed 26 August 2015.
[27] Curran Tom and Trahent Mark 'The Silence' *FRONTLINE* 19 April 2011 (online) <http://www.pbs.org/wgbh/pages/frontline/the-silence/> Accessed 26 August 2015.
[28] Tu Janet I 'NW Jesuits to Pay $166 Million to Abuse Victims' *Seattle Times* 31 March 2011 (online) <http://www.seattletimes.com/seattle-news/nw-jesuits-to-pay-166-million-to-abuse-victims/> Accessed 26 August 2015; Demer Lisa 'Jesuit Abuse Settlement Aims to Heal' *Anchorage Daily News* 20 November 2007 <http://www.bishop-accountability.org/news2007/11_12/2007_11_20_Demer_JesuitAbuse.htm> Accessed 26 August 2015.
[29] *In re Catholic Bishop of Northern Alaska* No. 08–bk–00110 (2009) 'Declaration of Bishop Donald J. Kettler in Support of Chapter 11 Petition and First Day Motions' Document 31.
[30] *In re Roman Catholic Church of the Diocese of Gallup* No. 13–13676 'Declaration of Bishop James S Wall in Support of Chapter 11 Petition and First Day Motions' Document 19 Section II: E–F.

As of July 2015, nine Catholic dioceses, three archdioceses and two religious orders in the United States (collectively, the 'Diocesan Debtors') have filed for bankruptcy protection under chapter 11 the United States Bankruptcy Code.[31] In each instance, financial liability to survivors of abuse is cited as the precipitating cause of the bankruptcy filing. Catholic dioceses and orders are independently organised under state corporate law, and like other corporate entities, may file for federal bankruptcy protection if there is a good faith concern of inability to meet obligations as they come due.[32]

The purpose of a chapter 11 case is the reorganisation of financial affairs to allow the debtor to exit bankruptcy and continue its affairs while ensuring equitable treatment for creditors.[33] Various commercial organisations dealing with liability related to tortious conduct have used bankruptcy protection.[34] In the mass tort context, debtor organisations argue that even liquidation may not provide as much total compensation or treat plaintiffs in as fair a fashion as a reorganisation proceeding is likely to. Some commentators argue that a chapter 11 case can be beneficial for many stakeholders in eliminating a race to the courthouse, providing a degree of equitable treatment for tort victims and ensuring a stream of future income to fund recoveries by keeping the organisation as a going concern.[35] Others argue that chapter 11 underfunds tort recoveries and allows for unjust transfers of wealth to shareholders.[36]

There is some evidence that for the Diocesan Debtor cases, the chapter 11 proceedings might actually provide procedural and outcome advantages for survivors. First, for those survivors who did not come forward until the case was filed, the bankruptcy case might lower the barriers to obtaining a legal remedy. There is no need for these survivors to initiate a lawsuit. It takes only a short form informing the court of the nature of their claim, and there are plaintiffs' lawyers providing advice about what needs to be done.[37] Except where a claim has been either reduced to judgment or otherwise settled, the claim to be filed will indicate that it is a disputed debt of an undetermined amount.

The lower barriers may have enabled more people to come forward in the Rural Dioceses. In Alaska, at the time the Diocese of Fairbanks filed its petition in bankruptcy, it

[31] The Diocesan Debtors are: (1) Archdiocese of Portland Oregon; (2) Diocese of Tucson Arizona; (3) Diocese of Spokane Washington; (4) Diocese of Davenport Iowa; (5) Diocese of San Diego California; (6) Diocese of Fairbanks AK; (7) Oregon Province of the Jesuits; (8) Diocese of Wilmington Delaware (October 2009); (9) Archdiocese of Milwaukee Wisconsin (January 2011); (10) Congregation of the Christian Brothers (April 2011); (11) Diocese of Gallup New Mexico (November 2013); (12) Diocese of Stockton California (January 2014); (13) Diocese of Helena Montana (January 2014); (14) Archdiocese of St. Paul and Minneapolis MN (January 2015).

[32] *In re Marsch* 36 F. 3d 825, 828 (9th Cir. 1994).

[33] See, for example, LoPucki Lynn 'The Nature of the Bankrupt Firm: A Response to Baird and Rasmussen's *The End of Bankruptcy*' (2003–4) 56 *Stanford Law Review* 645.

[34] See, for example, Spender Peta 'Blue Asbestos and Golden Eggs: Evaluating Bankruptcy and Class Actions as Just Responses to Mass Tort Liability' (2003) 25 *Sydney Law Review* 223.

[35] Smith Douglas G 'Resolution of Mass Tort Claims in the Bankruptcy System' (2007–8) 41 *UC Davis Law Review* 1613.

[36] As above.

[37] See, for example, Noaker Law Firm 'Only 3 Months Left to File a Claim in Archdiocese Clergy Sex-Abuse Bankruptcy Case' 24 April 2015 (online) <http://noakerlaw.com/only-3-months-left-to-file-a-claim-in-archdiocese-clergy-sex-abuse-bankruptcy-case/> Accessed 26 August 2015.

was aware of 150 plaintiffs who among them had filed 140 lawsuits against the diocese.[38] After publication in Alaska, by the time the bankruptcy case was coming to a close, 290 claims had been filed against the diocese asserting injuries from sexual abuse.[39] Presently, at least 336 complaints are acknowledged by the diocese as credible.[40]

Second, in contrast to individual actions in state courts, or even a class action, where the plaintiffs would necessarily be a fairly limited group — such as all having been abused by the same priest or some other commonality —there would be little or no attempt to take into account the concerns of claimants who had yet to come forward. In a bankruptcy case, all claimants are in the same forum with the organisation itself, all insurers or other sources of funding and all other stakeholders. In order for an organisation to exit chapter 11 bankruptcy successfully, a plan needs to be approved by a majority of claimants in a class of creditors whose claims are impacted by the terms of the plan.[41] For the Catholic dioceses, this means a majority of abuse claimants must approve.[42] In bankruptcy, unsecured creditors (the majority of unsecured creditors in the Diocesan Debtors are survivors) negotiate as a single body advised by bankruptcy professionals whose fees are paid by the debtor's estate.[43] Further, in Diocesan Debtor cases, there is usually also a professional representing the interests of survivors who have yet to come forward.[44] Finally, the confirmation of a plan of reorganisation by a bankruptcy court imparts a significant degree of finality — generally no claims relating to anything that occurred before the bankruptcy case was filed will be judiciable outside of how such claims are intended to be dealt with under the plan. But this finality also means that the bankruptcy court retains jurisdiction to enforce the terms of the plan and that the organisation has limited rights to appeal.[45]

3.0 Who Are Survivors?

People suffered sexual abuse by Catholic clergy in different contexts in part depending on their religion, race, ethnicity, gender and national origin. Many indigenous people in the US, Canada and Australia were abused while in the care of the State at a residential school.[46] Hispanic communities in the United States have a unique relationship with the Catholic Church which affects whether survivors come forward and how they are received

[38] *In re Catholic Bishop of Northern Alaska* above note 29.

[39] *In re Catholic Bishop of Northern Alaska* No. 08–bk–00110 (2011) 'Memorandum on Debtor's First Amended Disclosure Statement' p 1.

[40] Diocese of Fairbanks 'List of Perpetrators' 30 April 2013 (online) <http://dioceseoffairbanks.org/joomla/index.php/survivors-information/list-of-perpetrators> Accessed 26 August 2015.

[41] 11 USC § 1126(c).

[42] Marlar James M 'Confirming the Catholics: The Diocese of Tucson Experience' (November 2005) 11 *Norton Bankruptcy Law Adviser* 1.

[43] *In re Catholic Bishop of Northern Alaska* No. 08–bk–00110 (2011) 'Application to Employ Pachulski Stang Ziehl & Jones LLP as Counsel to the Official Committee of Unsecured Creditors' p 4.

[44] As above.

[45] As above.

[46] Daly Kathleen *Redressing Institutional Abuse of Children* Palgrave Macmillan New York and London 2014 chapter 2; Report of the Royal Commission on Aboriginal Peoples (1996) vol 1 chapter 10.

when they do.[47] Research on rates of abuse by Catholic clergy is inconclusive with respect to gender, race, ethnicity or other demographic markers. Yet, as will be discussed here, the dominant image of survivors of sexual abuse by Catholic clergy is that of a white boy.

3.1 *Perceptions of Survivors*

Survivors who lead advocacy organisations, serve as lead claimants in class actions and tell their stories publically have reported feeling a duty to come forward, implying that their social status renders them 'believable', and they make their stories public so that those who hold less social status might also be believed.[48] These advocates, including leaders of the Survivors' Network of those Abused by Priests, are predominantly white.[49] One site has a list of pictures of survivors that site visitors can click on to read each story. Of 32 pictures, perhaps four depict people who appear to be of a racial group other than white, eight depict women who experienced abuse and two depict women mourning the loss of their sons. The remainder are white men — a representation that is disproportionate in terms of the total population of the US, and likely even more disproportionate in terms of numbers of survivors.

In telling their stories, survivors make note of markers of success or respectability — having served in the military, been a police officer or attained professional or advanced degrees.[50] In Australia, one of the most publicised cases is that of John Ellis. Mr Ellis is educated, articulate and was a partner at one of the largest law firms in the world before bringing his claim to the Archdiocese of Sydney. The Royal Commission into Institutional Responses to Child Sexual Abuse held a public hearing on Mr Ellis's case, which had set legal precedent when the New South Wales Court of Appeal held that no defendant existed against whom Mr Ellis could effectively pursue a claim.[51] It is the only such hearing to date focused on a single survivor's experience. The other public hearings have all studied experiences of multiple survivors or an institution's history with abuse spanning years. Of those other hearings, a significant portion are dedicated to elite institutions.

[47] Martin Michel 'Catholic Sex Abuse Hits Home for Latinos' *NPR News* 19 July 2007 (online) <http://www.npr.org/templates/story/story.php?storyId=12098261> Accessed 26 August 2015.
[48] Balboni above note 20 at 87.
[49] Survivors' Network of those Abused by Priests: <http://www.snapnetwork.org/contact> Accessed 15 May 2015.
[50] See, for example, Furnish Mark 'You Are Not Alone' 12 October 2002 <http://www.bishop-accountability.org/resources/resource-files/timeline/2002-10-12-Furnish-YouAreNotAlone.htm> Accessed 26 August 2015; *Ford v Law*; *Gregory Ford et al. v Bernard Cardinal Law et al.* No. 02-04551-T1 (2003), Affidavit of John Doe 17 (16 July 2003) <http://www.bishop-accountability.org/ma-boston/archives/ShanleyMO_R/Shanley_MO_26_Affidavit_Ex15_09_R.pdf> Accessed 26 August 2015; Rom Louis 'Devotion and Deceit' *Times of Acadiana* 7 August 2002 (online) <http://www.bishop-accountability.org/news5/2002_08_07_Rom_DevotionAnd.htm> Accessed 26 August 2015; Newman Andy 'Abuse Victim is Suspicious About Timing of Apology' *New York Times* 11 April 2002 (online) <http://www.nytimes.com/2002/04/11/nyregion/abuse-victim-is-suspicious-about-timing-of-apology.html> Accessed 26 August 2015; Jones above note 10.
[51] *Trustees of the Roman Catholic Church v Ellis* 70 NSWLR 565 (2007).

Of the 10 public hearings held as of April 2015 with respect to an individual school or facility, at least three examined elite private schools.[52]

To understand why members of dominant social groups feature prominently in public portrayals of survivors, consider the difficulty of making public a claim alleging child sexual abuse. There is a reasonable fear of not being believed, being labelled an attention-seeker and even when believed, that the severity of the abuse or its impacts may be brushed aside. There are serious consequences to making public stories of abuse. Male survivors are often considered weak or themselves potential predators. Their sexuality may be questioned. Female survivors are often assumed to have coped with childhood sexual abuse by later promiscuous behaviour, and may even be blamed for the abuse. For those who assert their claims in a court of law, even when cases result favourably, litigation is difficult.[53] Survivors often find themselves ostracised or criticised by loved ones who either do not believe their stories or believe they should keep quiet.

Lytton shows that the way plaintiffs frame allegations in tort influences media depictions of clergy sexual abuse.[54] The success of tort actions for sexual abuse is often dependent on the 'believability' and the apparent 'innocence' of the claimant, as 'plaintiffs' attorneys frequently frame claims in terms of the familiar story of an innocent victim injured by uncaring and unaccountable corporate officers'.[55] Thus, to the extent that media sources and advocacy organisations paint a picture of survivors as primarily white men, this picture may reflect the framing devices used by plaintiffs' attorneys in litigation. Logically, then, plaintiffs in clergy abuse litigation cases may be primarily white men or attorneys representing multiple plaintiffs may choose to highlight the stories of their white male clients. Popular conceptions of survivors' identities are influenced by the stories given prominence, and it is worth considering whether those conceptions are accurate for the entire group of survivors, or how they impact who comes forward to seek justice. Baird's work on the intersection of race, morality and sexual violence in Western societies would suggest that cultural perceptions of white men and women as moral beings and non-white people as outside that morality serves to silence survivors of sexual violence who do not fit the wider perception of who is vulnerable and redeemable.[56]

3.2 *Lack of Research on Survivors*

Even as the picture presented of survivors is predominately white, middle class and male, those who come forward are themselves pointing to the more vulnerable,

[52] 'Case Studies' Royal Commission into Institutional Responses to Child Sexual Abuse (online) <http://www.childabuseroyalcommission.gov.au/public-hearings/case-studies> Accessed 26 August 2015.

[53] Fogler Jason M et al 'A Theoretical Foundation for Understanding Clergy-Perpetrated Sexual Abuse' (2008) 17 *Journal of Child Sexual Abuse* 301 at 314

[54] Lytton Timothy D 'Framing Clergy Sexual Abuse as an Institutional Failure: How Tort Litigation Influences Media Coverage' (2009) 36 *William Mitchell Law Review* 169.

[55] As above at 174.

[56] Baird Barbara 'Morality and Patriarchal White Sovereignty' (2009) 11 *International Feminist Journal of Politics* 372.

explaining feeling motivated to speak in order to make room for the voices of others.[57] There are no empirical studies that track attributes or identities of victims of sexual abuse by Catholic clergy or the rates of successful litigation broken down by such attributes — at least in terms of race, ethnicity, economic status or even where the abuse occurred. One widely cited study was commissioned by the USCCB (the 'John Jay Study'), which collected information from the dioceses and religious orders themselves.[58] Thus, it can only account for those people of whom the diocese had been notified by the survivor filing a claim or coming directly to the diocese. Even in the John Jay Study, however, there is no way to determine the characteristics of the survivor body other than gender and age at which the abuse began.

There is no study showing how many survivors have brought claims that ultimately fail in a court of law, much less the gender, ethnicity, race or other characteristics of those survivors compared to those whose claims succeed. Most commentators agree that the majority of survivors never report the abuse at all, and most who do report do so years or even decades after the abuse began.[59]

Even where data exists which provides some insight into rates of abuse, it is difficult to interpret. One widely cited finding of the John Jay Study is that 81% of victims of sexual abuse by Catholic priests were male.[60] This would seem to support the widespread belief that the problem is one of sexual abuse of boys by priests. It contrasts, however, with studies of sexual abuse of children more generally, which find that far more girls than boys are victimised.[61] Commentators explain this discrepancy by reference to the typical patterns of behaviour in Catholic organisations — priests are far more likely to spend time with boys, who may serve as altar boys, than with girls, but there is little behind this explanation other than speculation. The extent to which boys do outnumber girls in terms of victimisation by Catholic priests, religious and lay employees is unclear, and doubts in this regard have focused on the role of homophobia and the patriarchal nature of the Catholic Church in calling attention to the abuse of boys and discouraging girls from reporting.[62] While the vast majority of people coming forward to Catholic organisations are men, female survivors tell of support groups for women who speak of abuse by priests but have never come forward.[63] One former priest now advocating for survivors mused that women might be very unlikely to come forward because of patriarchal notions of virginity and womanhood, hypothesising that there might be far more

[57] Balboni above note 20 at 86–92.

[58] John Jay College of Criminal Justice *The Nature and Scope of Sexual Abuse of Minors by Catholic Priests and Deacons in the United States 1950–2002* United States Conference of Catholic Bishops, Washington D.C. 2004. Is this a report? If so, '2004' needs to be replaced with: Report (2004).

[59] Astbury Jill *Child Sexual Abuse in the General Community and Clergy-Perpetrated Child Sexual Abuse: A Review Paper prepared for the Australian Psychological Society to inform an APS response to the Royal Commission into Institutional Responses to Child Sexual Abuse*, Australian Psychological Society Ltd, Melbourne 2013 p 13.

[60] John Jay College above note 58 at 6.

[61] For example, Finkelhor David et al 'Sexual Abuse in a National Survey of Adult Men and Women: Prevalence, Characteristics, and Risk Factors' (1990) 14 *Child Abuse & Neglect* 20.

[62] Van Wormer Katherine and Berns Lois 'The Impact of Priest Sexual Abuse: Female Survivors' Narratives' (2004) 19 *Affilia* 53.

[63] Balboni above note 20 at 62.

female victims than accounted for in the available data.[64] It is not necessary to make any firm assertion about which gender actually makes up the majority of victims to believe that the current data is not sufficient for confidence in the actual rates.

3.3 *Intersecting Identities of Survivors*

Despite the absence of data, there is reason to believe that the actual body of victims of abuse by Catholic clergy in the United States may include high proportions of people whose experiences are affected by intersecting axes of disadvantage. This would include children who grew up in institutions and children living in poor, immigrant or minority communities where abusive priests were sent to avoid scandal in other areas. Just as Crenshaw and others showed how popular conceptions of domestic violence survivors affect the visibility of Black women as survivors, it may be that popular conceptions of survivors of childhood sexual abuse (conceptions influenced by the percentages of survivors who seek justice in civil courts) affect the visibility of many survivors of sexual abuse by clergy.

Intersectionality theory hypothesises that various axes of disadvantage, including gender, race, age, sexuality and social status, have varied effects on the success of plaintiffs in court cases, and that the effects will be different among those plaintiffs for whom multiple axes are present.[65] This theory is supported by empirical evidence that plaintiffs whose identities or legal claims inhabit an intersectional space are less likely to prevail in court than others.[66] Child sexual abuse, by definition, is inflicted upon children.[67] Children make up a social class with limited rights, in court their testimony is often not given much credit and they are socialised to obey the directives of adults. Trauma inflicted on children has long-reaching effects even well into adulthood.[68] Thus, victims will necessarily inhabit at least one position of marginalisation, leading to the question of whether other identities, including race, gender and economic status, affect the ability of victims multiply disadvantaged to seek or attain justice.

The perception of boys as the primary victims of clerical child sexual abuse is worthy of note because child sexual abuse has different impacts for boys and girls. Boys in patriarchal cultures which condemn homosexuality will experience shame, confusion and often serious social consequences for coming forward when abused by men. Girls may be blamed and experience shame for their own victimisation and risk distinct, but comparable, social consequences for having 'lost' their virginity or bearing a child outside wedlock at a young age.[69] Girls and boys are socialised to

[64] Author interview with Patrick Wall 2 June 2015 (on file with the author).
[65] Best Rachel Kahn 'Multiple Disadvantages: An Empirical Test of Intersectionality Theory in EEO Litigation' (2011) 45 *Law & Society Review* 991 at 1002.
[66] As above at 1009.
[67] Ravnbøla Camilla Ida 'Intersectional Discrimination Against Children: Discrimination Against Romani Children and Anti-Discrimination Measures to Address Child Trafficking' (2009) UNICEF Innocenti Working Papers.
[68] Finkelhor above note 61; Roberts et al 'The Effects of Child Sexual Abuse in Later Family Life: Mental Health, Parenting and Adjustment of Offspring' (2004) 28 *Child Abuse & Neglect* 525.
[69] Balboni above note 20 at 62–3; Fogler above note 53.

react to these different consequences that may prevent or facilitate coming forward in particular cultures. Perhaps, for example, girls who were impregnated, sent away to bear children given away for adoption and told that their lives would be ruined if they ever spoke of it are particularly unlikely to come forward.

It is likely that abusers target the most vulnerable of potential victims, children who are unlikely to be believed if they were to report the abuse.[70] Many stories shared by survivors detail how they were children of single parents or dysfunctional families. Survivors talk of coming from single parent homes, of growing up poor and of the cultural and religious elevation of the status of priests.[71]

One of the most powerful criticisms of Catholic leadership in dealing with abuse is that priests about whom reports of abuse were made would be moved from placement to placement, thus giving likely abusers access to children in new settings where communities would not be warned of the dangers. Indeed, many of those criticisms allege that known abusers were specifically sent to poor, immigrant, indigenous or other disadvantaged communities.[72] No comprehensive study has been conducted which would trace the history of those priests who are known to have been abusers and determine the socio-economic status of the neighbourhoods and communities into which these priests were sent.

The John Jay Study did track the rate of reports for 14 regions assigned by the USCCB, but in releasing its data, it randomised the regions. Thus, it can be determined that some regions have higher numbers of reports of abuse, but it cannot be determined which regions, much less the rates for any more precise geographical divisions. The study concluded that there was not a great deal of difference between regions, but the data might be interpreted otherwise. The various regions show average rates between 3% and 6% of priests in ministry, per diocese.[73] The difference between 3% and 6% is arguably significant, as are other differences between rates of reports between different regions described in the data.[74]

Patterns of abuse and victimisation crossed international lines. Data presented to the Royal Commission in Australia show that the largest numbers of survivors who have come forward (whether to the Royal Commission itself or in some other forum) were abused in 'out of home care.'[75] This means they were cared for by the State or a religious institution. Indigenous Australians in particular are many times

[70] Pfeiffer Sacha 'Geoghan Preferred Preying on Poorer Children' *Boston Globe* (online) 30 May 2012 <http://www.bostonglobe.com/news/special-reports/2012/05/30/geoghan-preferred-preying-poorer-children/69DE1kOuETjphwmIBcgzCM/story.html> Accessed 26 August 2015.

[71] 'Survivor of Emotional, Physical and Sexual Abuse' 13 February 2015 <http://www.snapnetwork.org/survivor_of_emotional_physical_and_sexual_abuse>; Accessed 26 August 2015; 'I was terrified. I froze' 13 February 2015 <http://www.snapnetwork.org/i_was_terrified_i_froze> Accessed 26 August 2015.

[72] Innes Stephanie 'Tucson a "Dumping Ground" for Abusive Priests' *Arizona Daily Star* (online) 23 February 2014 <http://tucson.com/news/local/tucson-a-dumping-ground-for-abusive-priests/article_99076313-f4df-5602-8a11-f50efd923736.html> Accessed 26 August 2015.

[73] John Jay College above note 58 at 30.

[74] John Jay College Research Team *Supplementary Report: The Nature and Scope of Sexual Abuse of Minors by Catholic Priests and Deacons in the United States 1950–2002* (2006) chapter 1. Above n 58.

[75] Finity Consulting Pty Ltd *National Redress Scheme Participant and Cost Estimates: Royal Commission into Institutional Responses to Child Sexual Abuse* 30 January 2015 p 22, 26.

more likely to have grown up in out-of-home care, and are more likely to have been abused, than are any other Australians.[76] In Canada, residential schools for First Nations children had very high rates of sexual abuse.[77] In the United States, we see high rates of abuse in Native American residential schools.[78] The research is consistent with Ireland, Australia, the United States, Canada and other places — people raised in orphanages or residential schools for poor or indigenous children suffered very high rates of child sexual abuse.[79]

Survivors and their advocates charge that when priests were transferred from a setting where they had been accused of abuse, they were frequently transferred to settings where the people they were meant to serve were poor, and often to communities with high proportions of subaltern racial and ethnic groups.[80] Statements of survivors often include their disappointment in learning that dioceses or orders knew of claims of abuse and wonder if they were deliberately sent to poor areas, areas with significant populations of minority groups, where complaints would not be heard, where victims would not be believed. 'The biggest thing that really pissed me off was that [the priest] had done this — allegedly, had done this before', a woman who had been abused from the ages of six to eight by a priest at a church on a Native American reservation was quoted as saying, '[a]nd he was put on the reservation because it's a reservation. Maybe the thought was: Little Indian girls would not say anything'.[81]

3.4 *Are Legal Justice and Visibility Connected?*

If, then, the perception of survivors as mostly white and male renders less visible survivors who do not fit that profile, what does that mean for access to the forms of justice available to different survivors? Across the race, class and gender differences among survivors it is worth analysing how the various types of legal procedures may differently affect people across intersections of identity. As discussed above, chapter 11 proceedings offer an example of how certain processes might facilitate access to legal process in ways that traditional civil litigation does not. In the Rural Dioceses, where the body of survivors who have come forward are primarily immigrant, Hispanic or Native American communities, do we see an unexpected path to justice even as public awareness is focused elsewhere?

The scandal in Boston was very public, but many survivors and community members lack confidence that things have truly changed. There have been large settlements, public scrutiny, changes in church policy aimed at protecting children, audits showing compliance with that policy and increased public awareness. Yet many survivors are deeply disappointed with the level of accountability and responsibility taken

[76] As above.
[77] Daly above note 46 at 39–41.
[78] Smith Andrea *Conquest: Sexual Violence and American Indian Genocide* South End Press Oxford 2005 chapters 2–3.
[79] Daly above note 46 at chapter 2.
[80] Demer Lisa 'Jesuit: Alaska No Hiding Place for Problem Priests' *Alaska Dispatch News* 15 January 2009 (online) <http://www.adn.com/article/20090115/jesuit-alaska-no-hiding-place-problem-priests> Accessed 26 August 2015.
[81] Tu above note 28.

by Church organisations and the efficacy of child protection policies. Further, there is a sense that money has corrupted the sense of community previously enjoyed among survivors bringing claims together, that assigning dollar values to experiences of sexual abuse is dismissive, especially while the amounts assigned are such a small sum in comparison to the great wealth of the Church. The Archdiocese holds large tracts of real estate valued in the millions or hundreds of millions of dollars.[82] In 2013, the Archdiocese took in over US$150 million in collections, and collected nearly the same amount in 2014.[83] It is not difficult to imagine how one of the 552 survivors who were part of the US$84.25 million settlement might feel knowing that the Archdiocese collects more than 150% of the settlement every year, even as the settlement did not so much as require the Archdiocese to admit fault.

The survivors in the Diocesan Debtor cases did not have a choice about whether or not the dioceses would file for bankruptcy. The dioceses would not have filed for protection if they had not seen an advantage for them in initiating it. Despite this, the chapter 11 process has some advantages when considering the prospect for redress for the survivor body. In addition to the accessibility issues discussed previously, the most rational goal for all stakeholders is typically to establish a mechanism by which claims will be evaluated and paid through the plan. Negotiating tactics will reflect that goal; each stakeholder seeking to obtain or preserve assets, advantages and other bargaining points. Survivors, dioceses and insurance companies benefit from the elimination of strategic and emotional costs associated with a race to the courthouse. This is not to say that the parties' interests are completely aligned or that the plan negotiation process is easy. However, there is little strategic advantage for the organisation to deny or question the truth of any particular allegation. The disputes will be about the amount the organisation should contribute to a fund for survivors, and the value of the organisation's assets.[84]

The plan process may also result in the reduction of variance between recoveries associated with piecemeal litigation. Any feasible chapter 11 plan would allocate a fund from which all survivor claims would be paid according to a matrix described in the plan. Survivors have a voice in determining how that fund and matrix are set up. Although the process of making individual awards resembles the arbitration process in Boston, perhaps survivor input into the process design (the plan of reorganisation may also have provisions for future funding sources for settlement trusts, as is the case for the plan confirmed in the Diocese of Wilmington, Delaware case[85]) may render the process less of a zero sum game.

Further, in many of the Diocesan Debtor cases, including the Diocese of Fairbanks and the Jesuits in the Northwest cases, (the Diocese of Gallup has yet to confirm a plan as of the date of publication), the parties agreed to a number of non-monetary

[82] 'The Catholic Church in America' above note 4.

[83] Archdiocese of Boston above note 13.

[84] Boswell Susan et al 'The Church in Chapter 11: The Lessons of the Catholic Diocese Cases' (2008) *American Bankruptcy Institute Conference Materials* (online) http://www.bishop-accountability.org/bankruptcy/general/2008_05_28_ABI_The_Church.pdf.

[85] *In re Catholic Diocese of Wilmington, Inc.* No. 09–13569 'Conformed Second Amended Chapter 11 Plan of Reorganization of Catholic Diocese of Wilmington, Inc. 28 July 2011.

provisions. These provisions include personal and public apologies, publication of survivors' stories, implementation of new prevention efforts, publication of names of credibly accused clerics, release of documents and symbolic acknowledgements of abuse.[86] These are remedies that closely mirror what many survivors have said they are seeking — truth-telling, acknowledgement of harm, enforced and credible policy changes, as well as financial remuneration.[87] These remedies resemble the kinds of remedies that one might imagine would result from restorative justice proceedings.[88] They appear designed to restore, to heal and to promote relationships between organisations, communities and survivors.

Of course, there are non-monetary provisions in more traditional settlement agreements as well. Survivors report they value this kind of relief.[89] In the non-bankruptcy context, however, survivors and advocates often complain that the dioceses fail to comply with non-monetary provisions.[90] Enforcement is easier to access in the bankruptcy context. The bankruptcy court retains jurisdiction to enforce the terms of the settlement.[91] Further, bankruptcy plans in most cases involve the appointment of a third-party trustee to oversee the claim process, and this third-party trustee is often also given authority to quickly and finally resolve disputes about the terms of the plan, including the sufficiency of implementation of the non-monetary provisions.[92]

4.0 Conclusion

As legal processes continue, it is important to pay attention to how different processes affect survivors across jurisdictions and identity. Observing the processes ongoing in the Rural Dioceses, as they compare with those involving other Diocesan Debtors and high-profile jurisdictions like Boston in terms of access to justice and the form remedies take will take further study. While observations and critiques formed on the basis of studying more prominent dioceses may apply to their smaller, more rural counterparts, it is important to consider distinctions among them. Research which pays attention to these differences, as well as the needs and experiences of all survivors, will contribute to understandings of the connection between the visibility of those needing justice and their access to it.

In this context, the public face of the survivor movement seems mostly white and middle class, leaving many survivors' stories at risk of being left untold. Intersectional

---

86 Curran and Trahent above note 27.

87 Clohessy David 'Victims Want Real Change from Pope' *Survivors Network of Those Abused by Priests* 16 January 2014 <http://www.snapnetwork.org/victims_want_real_change_from_pope> Accessed 27 August 2015; Balboni JM and Bishop DM 'Transformative Justice: Survivor Perspectives on Clergy Sexual Abuse Litigation' (2010) 13 *Contemporary Justice Review* 2.

88 Gavrielides Theo 'Clergy Child Sexual Abuse and the Restorative Justice Dialogue' (2013) *Journal of Church and State* 617.

89 Clohessy above note 87.

90 See, for example, *Walsh v Diocese of Kansas City-St Joseph*, 'Complaint for Declaratory Relief to Compel Arbitration over Breach of Contract' 6 October 2011.

91 11 USC 1112(b)(4)(N).

92 For example, Marlar above note 42; *In re Catholic Bishop of Northern Alaska* No. 08–bk–00110 'Debtors and the Official Committee of Unsecured Creditors' Third Amended and Restated Joint Plan of Reorganization for the Catholic Bishop of Northern Alaska' at 2.135.

feminist scholars have shown how mechanisms which fail to account for the voices of people who utilise them can frustrate the purpose of those mechanisms.[93] Where survivors are encountering different legal mechanisms it is worthwhile considering the ways in which the bankruptcy process, perhaps surprisingly, takes survivor voices into account. In contrast to the traditional civil litigation path, processes like bankruptcy may facilitate wider participation and allow for survivor voices to be heard in crafting plans which seek to address all those affected by the failures of a particular organisation to protect them when they were children. Those who suffered abuse say they need to be heard and believed, their concerns need to be addressed and they need for those who wronged them to acknowledge that wrong. Any path that shows some promise in this regard is worthy of further examination and study, and will be useful in evaluating the success of redress programs. In coming years, research on outcomes for survivors and their perspective on legal process, including differences among races, ethnicities, genders, sexualities and other social markers, will be critical to deeper understandings of how to attain justice.

[93] White Lucie E 'Subordination, Rhetorical Survival Skills, and Sunday Shoes: Notes on the Hearing of Mrs. G.' (1990) 38 *Buffalo Law Review* 1; Howe above note 6.

Giving Voice to Narratives of Institutional Sex Abuse

Shurlee Swain

Abstract. The announcement of Australia's Royal Commission into Institutional Responses to Child Sexual Abuse was the culmination of a long campaign by survivor groups to have their stories heard. Although this campaign, and the organisations themselves, date only from the last years of the twentieth century, institutional sexual abuse has a far longer history. This paper will seek to trace the evidence of sexual abuse back into the nineteenth century and ask why it took so long for survivors to have their stories heard. It will argue that while institutional responses to allegations of sexual abuse remained remarkably consistent over time, it was only in the aftermath of the feminist (re)discovery of child sexual abuse in the 1970s that survivors were able to access a language through which to understand and articulate their experiences. Without access to such a language enabling them to position themselves as victims of, rather than being complicit in, such abusive behaviours, survivors were ill-equipped to resist the attempts by those in authority to silence their concerns.

'All children deserve a safe and happy childhood', the charge to The Royal Commission into Institutional Responses to Child Sexual Abuse begins. It continues by recognising the nation's international responsibilities to protect children from all forms of abuse, before narrowing in on child sexual abuse as its exclusive focus.[1] In so doing, it follows a path which has become familiar both nationally and internationally. The (re)discovery of child abuse in the 1960s was, by the 1980s, overwhelmed by a focus on child sexual abuse, characterised as the most extreme transgression of the supposed innocence of childhood.[2] The emphasis on institutional child sexual abuse has brought into the spotlight religious organisations which played such a major role in the provision of out-of-home care for children and the degree to which this exposed them to the risk of clerical abuse. This paper aims to track this transition,

---

[1] New South Wales, Queensland, South Australia, Tasmania, Victoria, Western Australia. Royal Commission into Institutional Responses to Child Sexual Abuse. *Terms of Reference (2013)*. <http://www.childabuseroyalcommission.gov.au/about-us/terms-of-reference> Accessed 28 April 2014.

[2] Scott Dorothy and Swain Shurlee *Confronting Cruelty: Historical Perspectives on Child Abuse* Melbourne University Press Melbourne 2002 p 150.

explaining how the relationship between government and the churches functioned to both foster abuse and suppress its disclosure and exploring the ways in which the feminist analysis of child sexual abuse, articulated particularly in the work of Linda Gordon in the 1970s, helped to give victim/survivors the language through which to bring their experiences into the public domain.

Although the feminist concern was with the abuse of girls within the family home, the new discourse, adopted by predominantly male survivor/victims of extra-familial clerical abuse, built upon notions of childhood innocence which stood in sharp contradistinction to the libertarian analyses of child sexuality that had developed within both the women's and the gay liberation movements. Using the testimony presented to recent Australian inquiries, this paper seeks to trace the way in which this new discourse has been used by care leavers to name their experiences as abusive and to identify the failures in the systems charged with their care that allowed such abuse to occur. While such testimony does not give access to a factual account of institutional life, it does demonstrate the way in which the abuse was experienced and understood and how these understandings have changed over time. Through the analysis of this testimony the article is able to show how pre-existing conceptions of the children as morally tainted combined with a culture of denial amongst care givers, and the authorities responsible for their regulation and supervision, to create an environment in which abuse was able to thrive.

1.0 Inquiries into Past Welfare Practices

The beginning of Australia's series of public inquiries into past child welfare practices is usually dated to the National Inquiry into the Separation of Aboriginal and Torres Strait Islander Children from their Families which arose in response to evidence from the Royal Commission on Deaths in Custody of the impact of child removal on Australian Indigenous communities. The terms of reference made no mention of sexual abuse but in the evidence presented there were more than 502 instances noted, earning the phenomenon its own section within the final report released in 1997.[3] The two subsequent Federal inquiries, *Lost Innocents* and *Forgotten Australians*, followed a similar trajectory, with sexual abuse absent from the terms of reference but identified in the subsequent reports as prevalent in the institutions which housed child migrants and local children taken into care.[4] In the report of the inquiry into abuse in Queensland institutions completed in 1999, sexual abuse was considered as one of four forms of abuse that were found to be endemic in the system.[5] However, when South Australia instigated its own inquiry early in the new century the focus had narrowed, with sexual abuse positioned alongside deaths in care as the core

[3] Human Rights and Equal Opportunities Commission (NSW) *Bringing Them Home: National Inquiry into the Separation of the Aboriginal and Torres Strait Islander Children from their Families*, Report (1997) 162.

[4] Australian Senate Community Affairs References Committee, *Lost Innocents: Righting the Record* Report on Child Migration (2001) 75.

[5] Forde Leneen *Inquiry into Abuse of Children in Queensland Institutions* Report (1999) iv, 87.

subjects for investigation as indeed it became for the Victorian inquiry which reported in late 2013.[6]

Internationally a similar pattern prevails. Anne-Marie McAlinden identified three distinct periods in her chronology of inquiries into child welfare in Ireland. From the 1930s to the 1970s the focus was on the lack of basic care within institutional environments; from the 1970s to the 1990s attention turned to abuse within the family and the failure of child protection services; but from the late 1990s the paedophile priest claimed centre stage.[7] The Shaw Inquiry, which reported in 2008, dated the rise of concern about sexual abuse in relation to out-of-home care in Scotland to the 1980s, but noted that the issue itself was not new, documenting inquiries in other parts of the British Isles dating back to the 1940s. The distinction was, however, that these inquiries were conducted internally, and culminated with the offender being removed, but prosecution avoided in order to preserve the reputation of the organisation involved. 'Although sexual abuse was not a public concern at this time', the report concluded, 'it was still recognised that staff could be sexually attracted to children'.[8] The inclusion of a clause making it an offence for any member of staff to 'commit an act of sexual immorality' with children in their care in the 1913 Scottish *Mental Deficiency and Lunacy Act*, would suggest that this awareness was almost as old as the institutions themselves.[9]

The thin documentary evidence in the public domain in Australia points to a similar scenario. In 1875 Victorian newspapers reported the dismissal of the Geelong Orphan Asylum superintendent after the girl charged with 'tending his private apartments' was found to be pregnant.[10] Another staff member who had known of the pregnancy for three months without informing the committee was also dismissed, but nothing was noted as to the fate of the young woman.[11] In 1899 the superintendent of the Strathfield Institution for the Blind defended himself against charges of improper behaviour from several of the female residents. The offences had taken place five years previously and the superintendent's wife accused the now adult complainants of having ulterior motives in bringing the matter to public attention, saying: 'As you kept it to yourself so long you might have kept it altogether. You only tell me in order to break my heart'.[12] In 1900 Australian papers aired stories of the return to New Zealand of a Marist brother charged with five counts of indecent assault involving residents of a boys' reformatory in Stoke. The charges failed after:

[6] Mullighan Edward (South Australia) *Children in State Care: Commission of Inquiry: Allegations of Sexual Abuse and Death from Criminal Conduct* Report (2008); Victoria, Betrayal of Trust: Inquiry into the Handling of Child Abuse by Religious and Other Non-Government Organisations, *Final Report* (2013).

[7] McAlinden Anne-Marie 'An Inconvenient Truth: Barriers to Truth Recovery in the Aftermath of Institutional Child Abuse in Ireland' (2012) 33 *Legal Studies* 5 at 1.

[8] Shaw Tom *Historical Abuse Systemic Review: Residential Schools and Children's Homes in Scotland 1950 to 1995* Scottish Government Edinburgh 2007 p 28.

[9] As above at 60.

[10] Details of all the institutions mentioned in this article are available at http://www.findandconnect.gov.au/.

[11] 'General Items' *The North Melbourne Advertiser* 22 January 1875 p 2.

[12] 'Sydney Libel Action' *Western Mail* (Perth) 25 August 1899 p 28.

> the principal witness ... contradicted himself, and finally admitted having been guilty himself of similar offences upon his school-fellows ... The judge ... remarked that he could not punish a cat upon such testimony but the reformatory was removed from the Brothers' control.[13]

The evidence presented to recent inquiries suggests that these were far from isolated instances. In Queensland, Leneen Forde concluded, 'complaints of sexual abuse ... emerged in almost all of the institutions under consideration'.[14] South Australia's Mullighan report agreed:

> The alleged sexual abuse occurred in every type of care from the 1940s onwards, including institutional care (large congregate care in government and non-government homes up to the 1970s), smaller group care (cottages, hostels and youth shelters from the 1960s to early 1980s), residential care units (admission, assessment and community units from the 1970s to the present), foster care (placements with other families from the 1940s to the present), family care (placement on probation to live at the family home from the 1940s to the present) and in secure care facilities (from the 1950s to the present).[15]

Nor was this abuse unknown to the authorities, with a series of investigations conducted from the 1940s onwards, all of which were resolved internally, usually by the relocation of the children involved.[16]

2.0 Feminists and the (Re)Discovery of Child Sexual Abuse

The explanation for the silence around such instances of sexual abuse, American scholar Linda Gordon has argued, was the absence of a feminist voice, or a feminist consciousness, to provide the language through which concerns could be articulated. Without such a feminist voice, she suggests, the identification of instances of child sexual abuse served only to supply 'evidence and arguments for constricting and disempowering children'.[17] When complaints were investigated the focus was on the sexual knowingness of the child rather than the offender who was more likely to be seen as pathetic than predatory.[18] Gordon's article appeared as part of a feminist response to the 1987 Cleveland scandal in Britain, in which parents were found to have been falsely accused of abusing their children. The consequent inquiry, which provided support for calls to reduce the role of the State in relation to intra-familial child sexual abuse, threatened to reverse the gains that feminists believed they had made. Gordon's contribution, as an historian, was to show how, in the early decades of the twentieth century, 'powerful ideological tanks' had been able to render victims

[13] 'Stoke Orphanage Scandals' *Kalgoorlie Western Argus* 4 December 1900 p 37.
[14] Forde above note 5 at 87.
[15] Mullighan above note 6 at xiii.
[16] As above at 33.
[17] Gordon Linda 'The Politics of Child Sexual Abuse: Notes from American History' (1988) 28 *Feminist Review: Special Issue Family Secrets: Child Sexual Abuse* 61 at 56.
[18] Angelides Steven 'The Emergence of the Paedophile in the Late Twentieth Century' (2005) 36 *Australian Historical Studies* 278 at 272.

'invisible and mute', in the hope that a similar silencing of the incipient feminist voices of the 1970s would not reoccur.[19]

The feminist realignment of understandings of sexual abuse vigorously asserted the essential innocence of the child 'victim' and recast the offender as a transgressive character, threatening the entire notion of childhood. The transgressor, however, was no longer exclusively, or indeed predominantly, the evil stranger. The most dangerous place for the girl child, feminists argued, was, as it had always been, within the family home, made dangerous by the patriarchal power which it embodied. 'Child sexual abuse' needed 'a political interpretation … situating the problem in the context of male supremacy in and outside the family'.[20] Introducing the notion of power and powerlessness into the analysis, this reinterpretation reshaped contemporary understandings.[21]

In the 1970s, consciousness-raising groups had broken the silence around rape and incest providing a focus for early feminist research.[22] The first victim accounts of sexual molestation as a child came from women who were part of the feminist movement at this time and they empowered other victims, including men, to come forward.[23] Increasing media focus on allegations of sexual abuse in a range of community settings provided the space for a feminist analysis to enter into wider discourse. The dissemination and acceptance of this research saw child sexual abuse removed from the realm of individual pathology and acknowledged as a social and political issue demanding action from governments and the courts. Successful prosecutions recognised the credibility of the child witness, creating the opportunity for victims of institutional abuse to bring their testimonies of collective victimisation into the public domain. Although in the general community girls were and are far more likely than boys to be victims of sexual abuse, in the context of the inquiries the original narrative of girls abused by their fathers has been replaced by one dominated by boys abused by priests and other religious figures in institutional settings.[24]

The essentialism which arose from a feminist articulation of child sexual abuse has caused concern to scholars who argue that it has led inevitably to a further disempowerment in its failure to recognise children as sexual subjects. Sexuality scholar Steven Angelides identifies 'a significant reversal of the common twentieth-century tendency of victim blaming, [through which] the innocent, powerless, blameless, and

[19] Gordon above note 17 at 56.

[20] As above at 63.

[21] Angelides Steven 'Feminism, Child Sexual Abuse, and the Erasure of Child Sexuality' (2004) 10 *GLQ: A Journal of Lesbian and Gay Studies* 141 at 148.

[22] McIntosh Mary 'Family Secrets as Public Drama' (1988) 28 *Feminist Review: Special Issue Family Secrets: Child Sexual Abuse* 6 at 14.

[23] The first such disclosure was made in New York in 1971 by Older Women's Liberation Group member Florence Rush. For a discussion of this disclosure and its relationship to early feminism see Davis Joseph *Accounts of Innocence: Sexual Abuse, Trauma and the Self* University of Chicago Press Chicago 2005 p 29.

[24] Parliament of Victoria *Betrayal of Trust* above note 6 at 128; Daly Kathleen 'Conceptualising Responses to Institutional Abuse of Children' (2014) 26 *Current Issues in Criminal Justice* 5 at 9–10. There have been few attempts to explain the gender disparity that is noted by most inquiries however Parliament of Victoria *Betrayal of Trust* at 137 suggests that higher levels of recidivism amongst perpetrators who target boys may lead to more victims in institutional settings.

unconsenting "victim" and "survivor" of sexual abuse became key cultural terms'.[25] 'The discourse of child sexual abuse', he argues, 'has expanded at the expense of a discourse of child sexuality'. By focusing on issues of power and powerless, he concludes, feminist scholars have profoundly misunderstood 'the dynamics of human sexual and intersubjective relations' avoiding any analysis of some of the 'thorny issues of child sexuality'.[26]

Angelides does not suggest that this erasure of child sexuality was intentional but rather that in the face of rising concern about paedophilia and child sexual abuse the space within which it could be discussed shrank.[27] Australian feminist scholar Barbara Baird shares Angelides's concern, suggesting that child sexual abuse has gained such currency because it resonates with larger concerns about the viability of the nation. In the wake of the evidence of widespread sexual abuse brought to light in the series of child welfare inquiries, she argues, any instance of the sexualisation of children had to be condemned if the national virtue was to be restored.[28] However, in the process, the prominence given to the 'passive', 'innocent', victim child denied any space in public debate for 'the voice of children whose sexual experience may be more complicated than only victimisation'.[29] In reality, criminologist C.W. Gooren argues, 'the innocence/danger dichotomy is undermined by youngsters themselves ... hinting at the generality of paedophilic desire', and blurring attempts to draw a stark line between childhood and adulthood.[30] Yet to acknowledge such sexual agency is to undermine the many purposes, personal and national, which the assertion of childhood innocence serves.

3.0 Care Leaver Views

Such views are anathema to both campaigners against and victim/survivors of child sexual abuse for whom the notion of childhood innocence is critical to establishing their case. However, amongst care leavers and their supporters, there is a concern that with an exclusive focus on sexual abuse as *the* crime against childhood, other aspects of abuse disclosed by the inquiries are ignored. As Miss T. told the Forgotten Australians Inquiry: 'One of the problems state wards have is that society can relate to and understand sexual abuse. However there does not appear to be an appreciation of the effects of being ... in care'.[31] Allegations of widespread child sexual abuse in

[25] Angelides above note 21 at 142–3.
[26] As above at 150, 153.
[27] Angelides Steven 'What's Behind Child Sex Panics?' (2011) 2 *Lambda Nordica* 101 <http://www.lambdanordica.se/wp-content/uploads/2011-23-Angelides-Panics.pdf> Accessed 20 March 2015.
[28] Baird Barbara 'National Virtue and the "Media Sexualisation of Children" Discourse in Australia' (2013) 16 *Sexualities* 651 at 658–9.
[29] Baird Barbara 'The Resignation of the Governor-General: Family Drama and National Reproduction' (2009) 15 *Cultural Studies Review* 65 at 70–1.
[30] Gooren JCW 'Deciphering the Ambiguous Menace of Sexuality for the Innocence of Childhood' (2011) 19 *Critical Criminology* 29 at 30–1.
[31] Commonwealth. Conduct of Senate Inquiry into Children in Institutional Care, *Submission 214* (2004-7). Also available online at <http://www.aph.gov.au/Parliamentary_Business/Committees/Senate/Community_Affairs/Completed_inquiries/2004-07/inst_care/submissions/sublist> Accessed 7 January 2014. Those making submissions to the inquiry had the choice as to whether to use their own names, pseudonyms or remain anonymous. The submissions cited here reproduce the names

religious and other community settings created a sense of threat that was missing from the broader instances of neglect. The focus on sexual abuse also allowed abuse to be individualised, depicted as the action of psychologically abnormal individuals, and hence diverted attention from the degree to which abuse of all kinds was endemic within institutions which had been trusted to care, and hence from the extent to which society was complicit in what has now been shown to have occurred.[32] 'Sexual abuse is always highlighted as if it was the "worst" abuse', writes CLAN co-founder Joanna Penglase. 'What gets lost here is that children were violated in every sense in an institution, and being used sexually was just one of those violations.'[33] This argument for systemic abuse, in a system in which so many of the institutions functioned under religious auspices, has proven far harder to advance.

4.0 Sites of Vulnerability

Evidence presented to the various inquiries supports the claim for sexual abuse as a systemic rather than an individual problem. Rather than being built around idealised notions of childhood innocence, institutions for children were saturated with a sexuality, the presence of which was suppressed, or more often completely denied, confronting the residents with experiences which they had no language to describe, and against which they had little ability to protest. Boys commonly swam naked, and bath-times for both boys and girls were confusingly sexualised. As a small child at the Salvation Army home in Box Hill, Steve:

> wondered at why the person washing me took a lot of time washing my 'private parts' ... [with the result that] at times the routine of washing became very painful due to excessive rough handling.[34]

Relief only came when he was 'old enough to shower, and those episodes were placed and blocked in the back of my mind'. The showers at Mater Dei, Camden, Dianne W. recalls, had 'no doors and the nun would stand and watch us but teach us it was a mortal sin to look at each other with nothing on'.[35] For the boys at St John's Goulburn a similar situation prevailed:

> To look at yours or another body was a sin, and you only touched it if you went to the toilet. Anything else was filth, and a sin. [Yet] the nuns had no problem touching us to hit us, or to look at us in the showers, naked ... One nun came up to me when I was

attached to the original, except in the case of full names, where only the first name and initial is reproduced.

[32] Hawkins Russell and Briggs Freda 'The Institutionalised Abuse of Children in Australia: Past and Present' (1997) 133 *Early Child Development and Care* 41 at 42.

[33] Penglase Joanna *Orphans of the Living: Growing Up in 'Care' in Twentieth-Century Australia* Curtin University Books Fremantle 2005 p 145.

[34] Above note 31 Submission 510.

[35] As above Submission 193.

> about fifteen and told me I was developing very nicely. This was very embarrassing to a young boy that had been told that desiring the body was an offence.[36]

The public display of young naked bodies, John S. has come to understand, served as a 'smorgasbord' from which staff with paedophilic tendencies could select their next victims.[37]

Housed, and often also schooled, within closed institutions, children had a very limited understanding of prevailing sexual norms. There was much in the daily institutional routine that verged on the sexual. John B.'s experience at Melbourne's Methodist boys' home, Tally Ho, captures this confusion well. Taken to the superintendent's office:

> For corrective punishment — for what I know not. He took me on his knee and spoke gently as a daddy. Then came the punishment — ten strokes of the cane being prescribed ... As a prelude to the punishment the Captain would observe: 'My dear boy, this hurts me as much as it hurts you.' I found this hard to believe.[38]

The progression from the 'normal' to the criminal was subtle, leaving the isolated and uninformed child unable to resist. Having been brought up by nuns at Nazareth House, Sebastopol in the 1940s, Alan C. was shocked when he was introduced to masturbation by the older boys, but was reassured when he was told that that 'sort of conduct was practised by most of the managers'.[39] Fondled by a Salvation Army officer on a rare outing to a drive-in theatre in the 1960s, James N. was dissuaded from resisting by another resident, who told him 'it's all right, we all do it ... [he] won't hurt you', but fumbling in the car transformed into a full scale assault in his bed later that night, an incident he is still unable to relate.[40] Anally penetrated regularly from the age of ten, in his dormitory at the Salvation Army home in Box Hill, Brian C. had nothing against which to judge the situation, describing himself as being 'too young at the time to realise what was even happening'.[41]

Abusers played on the children's vulnerabilities. Barry M. self-identified as a sexually available 'bumboy'. Living at a Salvation Army home in the 1950s and 60s he was lured into one of the officer's room by the offer of treats:

> We never got Milo, biscuits or lollies at Riverview, so he knew how to lure me ... Each time I was tempted by the treats and hoped that the sexual abuse would not follow.[42]

---

[36] As above Submission 330.
[37] As above Submission 312.
[38] Bryant John *There Was a Man Whose Name Was John: An Autobiography* Self-published Perth 1982 p 5.
[39] *Forgotten Australians* above note 31 Submission 471.
[40] As above Submission 399.
[41] Family and Community Development Committee (VIC) *Inquiry into the Handling of Child Abuse by Religious and Other Non-Governmental Organisations*, Submissions (2013) available at <www.parliament.vic.gov.au.fcdc/article/1789> Accessed 29 March 2014.
[42] *Forgotten Australians* above note 31 Submission 75.

Comforted by one of the Christian Brothers after a severe beating at St Augustine's, Geelong, in the late 1950s, Bryan G. thought he 'had a friend, and as I had never been shown affection by another human being that I could remember, I welcomed it'. With the help of lollies, cigarettes and wine the relationship developed until Bryan was regularly abused in the brother's room. Although his initial reaction was to resist, eventually he 'got to the stage where I thought stuff it, I get a smoke and a drink of plonk, all I've got to do is whack him off'.[43] Only when he discovered that other boys were providing similar services but being paid more did he join with them to attempt to expose the offender. Obliging the abuser also brought an element of protection. At St Augustine's, Leslie B. recalled, 'the Brothers … had favourite boys … the sissy types [who] never got bashed like the rest of us'.[44]

Yet acquiescing was rarely a choice. What is striking from survivor accounts is the almost complete inability of institutionalised children to control access to their own bodies. When one of the officers at the Bexley Salvation Army Home took a group of boys on an outing in the 1930s, Jack H. found his pleasure quickly staunched:

> On the train he would spread his coat over his and our laps and start to touch us to arouse us. On arrival he would tell us to go for a nude swim, [but] he usually left one back, when he would begin his sexual abuse. He was insatiable.[45]

At St Vincent's, South Melbourne, Mark M. was assaulted by a brother to whom he had gone for medical treatment.[46] More commonly the intrusion came in the dormitory at night. At the Salvation Army home in Goulburn in the 1940s Ralph D. recalls officers touching boys in the genital area and watching to see what would happen, hitting the penis if it became erect.[47] Sent to St Augustine's in the 1950s, William D. came to realise that the dormitory was set up in a way which facilitated abuse:

> It was always the same. I would get out of bed to turn off the light, he would shut the door and start to fondle me … as he was fondling me he was moving towards his room. Once I was in the room he would shut the door.[48]

Regularly summoned from his bed at the Salvation Army Boys' Home at Nedlands in the 1940s Ernie T. was powerless:

> Waiting at night in bed was awful — I was so frightened that he would come and get me, and he did. Even if I faked being asleep he would shake me and I knew I had to get up or I'd get flogged.

[43] As above Submission 129.
[44] Above note 41.
[45] Forgotten Australians above note 31 Submission 411.
[46] As above Submission 38.
[47] As above Submission 282.
[48] As above Submission 227.

Initially too frightened to complain, later he was too ashamed so the 'abuse went on until they shoved me out of the home at 15 years old'.[49]

It was not only within the institutions that children were at risk. The practice of holiday hosting provided another source of danger. Mark McCabe, who was living at St Vincent's, South Melbourne, in the 1950s, came to believe that an annual picnic organised for the boys served as a 'meat-market' with 'some people ... selecting the boys they wished to billet out at Christmas ... [alleging] there was plenty of anecdotal evidence that boys were sexually assaulted during the Christmas holiday period'.[50] Abused by his holiday host in a caravan park shower block, Peter S. felt completely powerless:

> I had no knowledge of phone numbers of either my parents or house parents. Also, by this stage I had already learnt not to trust anyone and was wary of informing people of my abuse, as I was afraid it would only make things worse.[51]

Assaults both within and beyond the institutions were made even more confusing because they were committed in environments and by people who were overtly religious. Patrick Parkinson has observed that:

> the power and influence that clergy have can be used for great good or can be gravely misused. Since in religious communities, priests or ministers are influential in defining the boundaries of what is right and wrong, they have the power to define abusive behaviour as normal.[52]

Arguing that abuse has always been present in religious organisations, Fiona Hill points to ways in which 'the appearance of innocence' could be maintained by 'power games, including appeals to the Bible, and a range of strategies that ensured victims were silenced and marginalised'.[53] Children struggled to make sense of abuse which took place in sacralised spaces, the sacristy of the orphanage chapel for Margaret F. in the 1950s,[54] or, for Wayne L., in the 'red glow' emitted by the statue of St Vincent de Paul.[55] Abused children struggled to reconcile actions and words. 'In church every Sunday', one Kilmany Park resident recalled, 'we were told of this God of love and understanding who was watching over us. I could not understand, because I thought: "Jeez, what's happening? He's not watching over me".'[56] Every night, the brother who was regularly abusing Vincent D. at

---

[49] As above Submission 496.

[50] As above Submission 38.

[51] As above Submission 527.

[52] Parkinson Patrick 'What Does the Lord Require of Us? Child Sexual Abuse in the Churches' (2002) 4 *Journal of Religion and Abuse* 13.

[53] Hill Fiona 'Churches as Partners in Institutionalised Abuse: Disarming the "Bible-Bashers"' (2005–6) 18 *Women Against Violence* 5 at 5.

[54] Family and Community Development Committee (VIC) *Inquiry into the Handling of Child Abuse by Religious and Other Non-Governmental Organisations*, Transcript (2013) available at <www.parliament.vic.gov.au.fcdc/article/1786> Accessed 30 March 2014.

[55] Above note 31 Submission 15.

[56] Above note 4 at 46.

St Vincent's, South Melbourne, in the 1970s would 'say things in my ear like "God bless you", when he kissed me goodnight'. 'Why did he say that to me?' he now wonders. Was it an admission that he had 'hurt me or was he saying it was ok to do that to us?'.[57] In a confused account by an anonymous respondent who had been in care in a series of institutions in the 1960s and claimed to have been abused by priests in each location, abuse and religion were intertwined with the assault being accompanied by a recitation of the Our Father and the Hail Mary, as if to confer forgiveness in the very midst of the sinful act.[58]

5.0 Silencing Mechanisms

This quasi-religious sanction also made it difficult for children to report abuse. The state entrusted children to the care of these organisations because they were religious and hence assumed to be above reproach.[59] The level of trust was such that inspection was minimal leaving children with virtually no-one outside the institution to whom they could speak.[60] Even in cases where children or their families attempted to speak out, they were unlikely to be believed. McAlinden has labelled this phenomenon 'social denial' grounded in a 'culture of disbelief' around clerical abuse.[61] Silence also prevailed within religious organisations where a belief in the sanctity of suffering and the power of forgiveness acted against the recognition of such behaviour as a criminal offence and the decision to act accordingly. Through this process the abuser became the victim, and the survivor was rendered un-Christian for demanding justice rather than offering forgiveness.[62]

Steve understood this dynamic and never thought to disclose the Salvation Army officer's behaviour: 'I was so scared at what would happen to me if I told anyone, no-one would believe me as I was only a child and they were trusted officers'.[63] The boys assaulted from around the age of ten by the dairyman at St John's Goulburn felt powerless for to alert the nuns was to confess to 'committing sexual acts and then being bashed for it'.[64] Others were more trusting. Margaret F. reported her assault to the sister in charge, only to be called 'a liar and a wicked, wicked child' and threatened with severe punishment if she raised the matter again.[65]

Ralph D. is adamant that such reactions arose out of denial rather than disbelief. The officers at his Salvation Army home, he argues:

> would have witnessed the exploitation, the bashings, the caning, the deprivation of sleep, the exhaustion from overwork, the withholding of food, the silence torture, the standing at attention in line torture, the sexual abuse, the sexual embarrassment and the many other ways that a child can be abused yet no-one intervened.[66]

---

[57] Above note 31 Submission 371.
[58] As above Submission 419.
[59] Forde above note 5 at vii.
[60] As above at 102.
[61] McAlinden above note 7 at 22–3.
[62] Hill above note 53 at 6.
[63] Above note 31 Submission 510.
[64] As above Submission 330.
[65] Above note 54.

Bryan G. recalls that when the boys at St Augustine's attempted to expose an offending brother, the reaction was swift. Addressed by the superintendent they were told:

> 'There is a rumour going round ... [and] if I hear one more word of it you will be up before the court on a charge of defamation of character, and you will be sent to Royal Park'. His parting shot, 'Who would believe you toe rags'.[67]

Complaining to the police after being assaulted at St Vincent's, South Melbourne, Mark M.'s experience confirmed the superintendent's judgment. When he finally absconded and went to the police, he was 'thrown in the wet-cell' with the drunks, punched by a detective and told 'not to bother coming to the Police Station with such cock and bull stories' and then returned to the custody of his abuser.[68]

Even where children were able to have their accusations heard outside the institution, the officials to whom they spoke colluded in dealing with the complaint internally rather than risk damage to the reputation of the church and indirectly of those who had entrusted children to its care. When Wayne L. finally absconded, his injuries were sufficient to persuade the police of the truth of his story. The detective took him back to St Augustine's and demanded to see the offender:

> [As the brother] came through the swinging doors, he was met with the sergeant's big fist. This laid [him] on the floor ... The burly copper stood over him and warned of further repercussions if he ever saw another boy in the condition I was in.

While Wayne was 'free of this creep sexually' he still had to live with what he described as 'his perverted revenge' and no charges were laid.[69]

Wayne L.'s experience is indicative of the degree to which external authorities were complicit in preserving the reputation of religious institutions. The pattern that emerges from the evidence given to the various inquiries is confirmed in institutional files. In some cases where children reported abuse, they noticed that action was taken. An offending staff member left suddenly or was relocated to another area of the home where they were less likely to do damage.[70] Sometimes a note was placed on file barring the accused from further interaction with children, but no-one gave an account of institutional authorities ever contacting the police.[71] Departmental files confirm that in cases where complaints had been made to external authorities, their first recourse was to go back to the institution to seek a resolution. If the offender was a staff member, the superintendent or matron was usually able to resolve the matter by a quiet dismissal. In cases where the superintendent himself was at fault, board members or church authorities stepped in to ensure that he was quickly removed. In the few instances where the state department referred the matter to police, the cases seldom progressed because police doubted that the evidence of the

66 Above note 31 Submission 282.
67 As above Submission 129.
68 As above Submission 38.
69 As above Submission 15.
70 As above Submission 473.
71 As above Submission 374.

victims would be believed in a court. Without witnesses, it was assumed, the word of a child would not stand up against the word of a respected adult for whom the loss of the position was considered to be sufficient punishment.[72]

6.0 Institutionalised Children as 'Moral Dirt'

In all of these discussions, the eye of pity fell upon the abuser, perhaps a once trusted former colleague now faced with disgrace, and the impetus was to minimise that harm. The focus was on providing opportunities for the sinner to repent rather than pursuing justice for the child. But, as Parkinson has persuasively argued, forgiveness in such cases became 'a spiritual argument for avoiding the consequences of the crime, and negating the need to deal with his offending behaviour'.[73] In order to understand the indifference to the child it is helpful to invoke Harry Ferguson's argument about institutionalised children as 'moral dirt'. The harsh treatment which such children received, he writes, was not aberrant but essential to the purpose of child rescue. Removed children:

> were treated harshly *because* they were victims of cruelty ... the key to unravelling the meaning of child abuse and institutional care lies in understanding the concept of neglect and its links with sexual morality and the notion of 'moral danger'.[74]

At the Melbourne Orphanage in the 1940s and 50s, any overtly sexual behaviour was read as evidence of 'moral degeneracy'. This judgment was clearly internalised by Doug McNeil who, when he could not rid himself 'of the pleasurable thoughts associated with' the sexual abuse he received in the Melbourne Orphanage, became convinced that he was indeed a 'filthy guttersnipe ... loathsome swine ... and vermin' and deserving of the punishment administered to him.[75]

7.0 Coming Out as Victims

The feminist reconfiguration of child sexual abuse gave care leavers the language and the tools to challenge this self-understanding. The identification of abuse as an exploitation of adult power which represents a major breach of trust provided the means through which victim/survivors, in their emerging support groups, could come to a new understanding of their experiences. These support groups brought care leavers into an alliance with the much wider groups of adults abused as children in other church and community sectors adding to the valency of sexual abuse as the greatest transgression of childhood innocence. Whatever the circumstances in which the sexual interaction occurred, they were children, and hence, by definition, were unable to give informed consent. By 'coming out' as victims, care leavers were able

[72] Information comes from institutional files held in the Victorian Department of Human Services archives. Access covered by confidentiality agreement, on file with the author.
[73] Parkinson above note 52 at 14–15.
[74] Ferguson Harry 'Abused and Looked After Children as "Moral Dirt": Child Abuse and Institutional Care in Historical Perspective' (2007) 36 *Journal of Social Policy* 123 at 131–2.
[75] McNeil Doug *Order of Things* Bentleigh 1995 p 17–18.

to access the self-help groups which played such an important role in the social activism of the 1970s and beyond, or to create self-help groups of their own around a similar model.[76] Blending emotion and policy these groups functioned to change both the inner world of the individual and forced the larger social world to confront their issues.[77]

While the testimony given before the various inquiries encodes much of the childish helplessness with which care leavers encountered the original abuse, it also provides evidence of the ability to reframe such experiences in line with this new vocabulary. The evidence is shaped by what Ahmed and Casey have labelled 'testimonial culture' which allows for a reworking of 'autobiography, confession and remembrance'.[78] Testimonies, Rosanne Kennedy reminds us, are never simple representations of the past, but rather function as 'social utterances which intervene in a present social context', addressing what Bain Attwood has called 'the past's residue in the present rather than … the pastness of the past'.[79] Central to that residue is the dysfunction in individual lives for which the public naming of sexual abuse can now give an explanation.

The glimpses of this new understanding are evident in the testimonies in several ways. Often it surfaces in angry outbursts which employ post-1970s terminology to condemn past abuse. Having described how the Colebrook Home in South Australia became 'a haven for sexual deviants' after its founders retired, Ruby H. slips into a human rights discourse, arguing that 'as children we were robbed of our personal rights'.[80] The publicity surrounding the exposure of offenders within the Catholic Church allows children who grew up in its institutions to link individual prosecutions to their experiences. Rosemary B., for example, cites the findings of the Forde report to validate her claim that the Church chose to hide paedophile priests in its children's homes. 'We accepted it was their right', she argues, 'for we knew nothing else. Nobody from the State Children's Department cared what was happening to us'.[81]

The new understandings are also evident when care leavers use their submissions to reflect on the damage that they have come to believe their abuse has caused. Now describing himself as 'homosexual (from birth I assume)', John L. admits to eventually welcoming sexual advances, but believes that the shame that accompanied such behaviour led him into increasingly anti-social activity and violent crime.[82] For Ann T., the new vocabulary provides little consolation. Identifying as one of those 'who were

[76] Whittier Nancy *The Politics of Child Sexual Abuse: Emotions, Social Movements and the State* Oxford University Press Oxford 2009 p 68.
[77] As above at 208–14.
[78] Ahmed Sara and Stacey Jackie 'Testimonial Cultures: An Introduction' (2001) 5 *Cultural Values* 1 at 1.
[79] Kennedy Rosanne 'The Affective Work of Stolen Generations Testimony: From the Archives to the Classroom' (2004) 27 *Biography* 48 at 49; Attwood Bain 'Settling Histories, Unsettling Pasts: Reconciliation and Historical Justice in a Settler Society' in Manfred Berg and Bernd Schaefer (eds) *Historical Justice in International Perspective: How Societies are Trying to Right the Wrongs of the Past* Cambridge University Press Cambridge 2009 p 217 at 236.
[80] Kartinyeri Doris *Kick the Tin* Spinifex Press North Melbourne 2000 p 54.
[81] Above note 31 Submission 202.
[82] As above Submission 210.

unlucky enough to be singled out as "the chosen ones" of the priests, nuns, lay workers and the older girls ... who picked us out to sexually abuse', she believes that she is 'scarred ... for life ... [adding] no amount of counselling can cure ... the pain I feel within'.[83]

For all its despair, Anne T.'s use of the term 'chosen one' is indicative of a buying into a new and shared identity created initially by the post-1970s understandings of sexual abuse, and consolidated through the investigations of institutional abuse in the years since. For one former resident of the Melbourne Orphanage the possibility of this new identity creates confusion:

> Everybody always asks me if there was any sexual abuse while I was at these places 'as a ward of the state' ... nowadays everybody knows this 'sex abuse' as a crime against society. When you're a child in the fifties and sixties you don't know much about this type of stuff ... I have memories and can tell certain things if I feel that I should, but I wonder what really happened and how much is fabricated as in a dream or in the mind because society says it must have happened. I really don't think I'm that sure of details and specifics of another life and time or at least not sure enough to state a fact without fear of error.[84]

Others have no such doubts. Child migrant, James A. M., describes the environment of the Christian Brothers' homes to which he was transported quite simply as 'the kingdom and reign of a paedophile'.[85] William A. validates his testimony simply by positioning himself of an inmate of 'the notorious Neerkol orphanage'.[86]

8.0 Conclusion

The reassertion of childhood innocence that was central to the 1970s feminist (re)discovery of child sexual abuse has provided care leavers with a valuable discursive tool in their struggle for redress. While its closure of a space in which to discuss childhood sexuality is proving problematic, that is an issue for the present which has little relevance for people dealing with residues of the past. Long after the redefinition of sexual abuse as an issue of patriarchal power has slipped from the centre of feminist debates, care leavers and other child abuse victims have been able to use such arguments to shame religious authorities, displacing them from their central position as guardians of national morality. This displacement was vividly demonstrated at the 2013 Victorian Inquiry when the Catholic Archbishop of Melbourne, Denis Hart, replied to accusations that the Church had not responded to abuse victims by remarking 'People will make their own minds'. Committee member Andrea Coote replied: 'The victims have made up their minds. They do not believe what you are saying'.[87] The shift from people to victims is crucial, for while the Church continued to appeal to an understanding still widely believed within the male clerical hierarchy and their almost exclusively male advisors, its representatives misunderstood the

[83] As above Submission 410.
[84] As above Submission 465.
[85] As above Submission 34.
[86] As above Submission 219.
[87] Above note 54 on 20 May 2013.

degree to which the victim voice has now become the dominant discourse shaping contemporary understandings of clerical abuse.

This article has argued for the importance of feminist discourses around child sexual abuse in enabling victims of institutional abuse to find a language in which to reconceptualise their experiences in out-of-home care. In so doing it has allowed them to discredit the attitudes that prevailed during their childhood that looked-after children were morally inferior, and that the predominantly religious organisations that had responsibility for their care were above reproach, an attitude which simultaneously exposed such children to higher risks because of the lack of official oversight and discredited any attempts they made to bring attention to their abuse. While the language of victimhood may come at a price it has given care leavers in Australia and beyond a powerful position from which to capture the attention of governments, to narrate their experiences of abuse and assert claims for redress.

Index

For Product Safety Concerns and Information please contact our EU
representative GPSR@taylorandfrancis.com
Taylor & Francis Verlag GmbH, Kaufingerstraße 24, 80331 München, Germany

www.ingramcontent.com/pod-product-compliance
Ingram Content Group UK Ltd.
Pitfield, Milton Keynes, MK11 3LW, UK
UKHW050753180926
475701UK00007B/1028